The Answer to Life

The Simple Solution to the Problems of Living

Brian Back

Table of Contents

Acknowledgements

Firstly, to my old friend Michael, who first told me and then showed me, by example, what the answer to life was. Thank you so much mate.

For Nic, whose unfailing enthusiasm, encouragement and support had a lot to do with getting this project off the ground.

For Sian, who read the whole thing and was massively praising and encouraging, even when it was way too long and incredibly amateurish.

For Toni, for your encouragement and great example. For Lloyd, for your excellent analysis and advice. For Nathan, for your expert opinion

For my old and great mate Neil, for his inspiration and encouragement, along with his excellent team at Fitzpatrick Design, for their perfect work on the book cover, producing exactly what I'd envisaged. For my other very old and great mate, Darryl, for his unfailing friendship and encouragement.

For Reece – told you I would! Thanks mate ☺. For Amanda, another college-mate, who, like Reece, read the whole thing and was kind and encouraging when I needed it.

For my very good friend Paul, who also slogged through the long unedited version – thank you!

Lina, whose comments on the nearly-finished version kept me going when I was seriously flagging. For Colin, for his unfailing support and encouragement.

For everyone at Biodanza, for always showing me the best example of how to live

For Fie, for listening to the whole rubbish original version and then being thoughtful enough to gently nudge me towards a much-needed editor.

For the patient, kind and incredibly useful editorial help of Claire Williamson, who did so much to push me and the book in the right direction.

For Graham, whose robust criticism firmed my resolve and helped drive me to the finish.

For Sam Jordison, for his insightful and encouraging work on the manuscript.

For Amanda, for her massively appreciated (by me) and undervalued (by her), but extremely useful analysis – I owe you a lot more beer Manda!

For Jordan, at Cobra Music Studios in Newport, for his excellent work on the recording and production of this audiobook. I definitely couldn't have done it without you. Thank you mate.

Last, but never least, for Rebecca, who's had to live with this book, and me, and has done so without complaint, always unfailingly showing me what the answer to life was

Introduction

There *is* an answer to life.

It's true; there is an answer - a way of thinking and being which makes sense of your life, gives it meaning and purpose, and creates a much better environment for everyone.

And when I say it's true, I mean it's 'The Truth' that's shared by all the major schools of thought which seek the answers to the human condition: in psychology, sociology, philosophy, throughout literature, legend and mythology, and in all the major religions and spiritual beliefs across the world and throughout our history.

Discovering this truth transformed my life. It's greatly improved all my relationships, enhanced my performance at work and made life much more fulfilling and worthwhile. But it took years of reading and research to find this truth - to trace the common thread that wove through all these different schools of thought. Inspired by what I'd learned, I went looking for the book that tied it all together. I wanted to buy, or recommend it to my family and friends, so they could experience the same improvements in their lives.

But I couldn't find it. It didn't exist. That's when I realised; I had to write it myself. I *had* to try and share what I'd found, so that maybe other people could change their lives too. Because everyone has the power and potential within them to transform and grow.

You have this power.

This book aims to help you on that journey, by persuading you through a combination of personal experience, theory and practice.

Trigger warning: Some of the events I describe in Chapter 1 may trigger an unpleasant emotional response, particularly if you've experienced anything similar in your own life. It's only Chapter 1 which contains this kind of content. The following chapters have an entirely different flavour, focusing on theory and learning, woven together with anecdotes.

Please note: As you progress through the book, you'll notice that some key ideas, messages and phrases are repeated. This will help you to install the information in your long-term memory. As you practice thinking and behaving in the ways which this book suggests, these will eventually become your automatic responses to life, assisting you in your journey to become the best that you can be.

Applying the ideas in this book has improved my life immeasurably. It's my sincere wish that they'll do the same for you.

Brian Back

Chapter 1: Why Listen to Me?

I'm no guru. I'm not the perfect picture of peace and enlightenment.

Peace has been hard to find and enlightenment an impossible dream. Life's often been difficult, so consequently, *I've* often been difficult. It's those difficulties that brought me here. Out of necessity and sometimes, desperation, I've been forced to search for solutions to the problems of living. But if you're reading this because you've struggled and you're looking for answers, then I think that's what you want to hear - that I've been there and 'paid my dues'.

Life got difficult pretty early for me. When I was seven, I threatened to kill my mum with a knife.

I'd been living in a state of constant fear. I never knew when the violence would come, only that it would. There was no pattern or warning; it could come at any time. She beat me regularly, randomly and repeatedly. She'd hit me with her fists, her feet, with a walking stick, a golf club - anything she could lay her hands upon. And then, if I started crying, she would scream:

'Stop crying or I'll give you something to cry about!'

We were in the kitchen when it happened. She'd suddenly exploded in one of her violent rages, foaming at the mouth, shouting, swearing and spitting curses at me. I was backed up against the sink, next to the kitchen drawers. She was *possessed*, fists clenching and unclenching convulsively as she came for me. And she was getting closer; close enough now for me to feel her rabid spittle land on my face, almost close enough to hit me. Without any conscious thought, I whipped round to the drawer next to me and tore it open. I snatched out the big carving knife, slashed it through the air in front of me and screamed, 'If you touch me, I'll kill you!'

And then suddenly, just like that, it was all over - the attack was over and her reign of terror had ended. I'd done it! I'd stopped it, all on my own.

Her face transformed – the snarl was gone. Her mouth dropped open and tears filled her eyes. Now overcome and overwhelmed with remorse and pity, she whispered: 'My God! What have I done to you?'

She never hit me again after that.

It's not a solution that I'd recommend, but I was desperate - I was fighting for my life. I knew her rages weren't just violent, they could be deadly. I'm the middle child, sandwiched between two sisters, but I should've had an older brother. I didn't though, because my mum killed him when he was eighteen months old. She shook him to death. She told me about this many times. She told me how she shook him and shook him and shook him and shook him, because he wouldn't stop crying. But the more she shook him, the more he cried, so in her rage, she just shook him even more. She shook him until he choked on his own sick and died. She somehow wasn't held responsible for his death though, so she was free to then have more children who she wasn't fit to be around.

It took many years for me to forgive my mum, although I managed it in the end. The forgiveness came when I was able to understand that she was herself a victim of childhood trauma. She was a product of her childhood experience, just as I am. She was adopted and her mother subjected her to levels of abuse which were even worse than my mum had inflicted on me. For example: her mother used to lock her in her room for days at a time, without allowing her out to eat, or even to use the toilet; she had to urinate and defecate in her bedroom, on the floor. When her mother would see this, my mum would be made to clean it up - by eating it.

Forgiveness is just a tiny part of the process of healing though, which for victims of childhood trauma is a lifelong process. If we go through repeated trauma in the vital formative years of our childhood development, it leaves us scarred and marred, because it fundamentally changes us. It changes the way we think and feel, changing the way our brain functions and therefore altering the way our body works.

The hugely important 'Adverse Childhood Experiences Study', undertaken by Dr Vince Felitti and Dr Bob Anda, very effectively demonstrates this. The study established undeniable correlations between adverse childhood experiences (ACEs) and poor health outcomes. It showed how ACEs affect brain development, immune systems and hormones, and make us much more susceptible to major health conditions affecting the heart and lungs. For example, it showed that if you have an ACE score of four or more (as I do), then you're two and a half times more likely to contract hepatitis or COPD, four and a half times more likely to become depressed, and twelve times more likely to commit suicide (1).

But although my childhood scarred me, it was also what drove me. You may find this too, that what can come out of trauma is a drive for change, to face up to what feels hopeless, and face down the despair.

Sometimes, I don't know why I kept going. It may be the most important choice we ever have to face; do we give up - because all seems hopeless, or do we keep going; keep hoping - despite there seemingly being no hope or possibility for change?

Jordan Peterson, in his global bestseller, *'12 Rules for Life'* (2), has an explanation for this persistence which makes sense to me. He states that it's our limitations in life which make it meaningful, because if we were all-powerful and all-knowing, then there would be nothing to achieve; there would be no challenges to rise to, therefore life would have no purpose or meaning.

From that perspective, I can now say that in some ways, maybe I've been kind-of lucky, because life brought the challenges that forced me to grow. I've travelled around the world, been employed in lots of different and interesting jobs, and done some enjoyable and worthwhile work.

It might be true to say that I managed this in spite of my childhood experience. But, I've come to see that my life has very much been a response to that experience – a search for what was missing, because of my childhood. It's because of my childhood experience that I was driven to do as much as I could and learn as much as I could about the meaning, purpose and 'answer to life'.

In that search for understanding, '*The Body Keeps the Score*' (3) by Bessel Van Der Kolk provided some answers. Van Der Kolk is an expert in the field of childhood trauma, with over thirty years' experience treating and researching its effects. His book demonstrates how childhood trauma is the cause of most mental illness and that mental illness is always also physical illness. The two are inextricably linked, as whatever affects the mind, affects the body, as the aforementioned 'ACE' study showed. This explained and made sense of some key aspects and events in my life.

Our experiences in childhood shape our reality. In the crucial developmental period of childhood, our brains are working hard to gain an understanding of the fundamental rules of our world. So, in childhood, if you were always in danger, the brain will be altered and re-structured to deal with a world which is always dangerous.

I've always had trouble sleeping. When I was a young child, I was too scared to go to sleep, because I never knew if, or when, my mother might suddenly burst in and attack me. I'd wrap myself up in my bedcovers, with only my mouth and eyes uncovered. I'd then rock from side to side, saying over and over 'happy and good, happy and good', trying to convince myself that I actually was happy and good. If I was, that surely meant I couldn't have done anything wrong, so I was safe. I'd repeat this mantra until I exhausted myself and eventually fell asleep. Although I'm no longer scared to go to sleep, because my conscious brain knows I'm not in danger, the primitive part of my brain, which is primarily responsible for survival, isn't reachable by conscious thought. That part of my brain doesn't want me to sleep. It wants me always awake and alert, because it learnt in childhood that danger is always present.

This primitive part of our brains, known as the amygdala, is responsible for the survival responses of 'fight, flight, or freeze'. It's more powerful and faster-acting than our conscious mind - it has to be, so that it can instantly take control and keep us alive when danger threatens. You'll have experienced this yourself many times. For example, if you're walking and talking with a friend and are about to cross a road without paying much attention, if a car horn suddenly beeps next to you, your amygdala will instantly take control and stop you in your tracks - without any conscious thought or deliberate action on your part. Your conversation with your friend will instantly cease and your enjoyment of the scenery will evaporate. Everything will be stopped, as the amygdala overrules all other brain functions and activities, in order to keep you alive.

The amygdala keeps me awake. And when I'm awake, it keeps me on alert and running on adrenaline - always rushing and panicking that I'm going to be late, or that I might in some way have done something 'wrong', which signals danger to my amygdala. This is known as 'hyper-vigilance'; it means that I'm always unconsciously vigilant and alert for danger at any moment. This unremitting alertness means that I'm very frequently tense and clenched in many of my main muscle areas - an effect of childhood trauma known as 'armouring'. Armouring often leads to trauma survivors experiencing tightness and damage to the hips. I had to have operations to have both of my hips replaced in my early forties, which is very young compared to the usual post-retirement age of most people who require this surgery.

Although these things have had a significant impact on my life, it's my romantic relationships which have been most affected by my childhood experience. Van Der Kolk states that it's only possible to be in an emotionally intimate relationship if we can let down our psychological, physiological and emotional defences with our partner. This means relaxing our natural vigilance, deactivating the survival mechanisms of the amygdala, thereby enabling our social engagement systems to function. That's been almost impossible for me. I eventually realised, after sabotaging another relationship, that the way I was unconsciously trying to overcome the hyper-vigilance was through sex. It was only after having sex with my partner that my defences dropped and I was able to feel relaxed and safe enough to emotionally connect with her. I wasn't consciously aware of this though, I just knew that I always felt an urgent need to have sex when I was with her. But this led to problems - led to my partner thinking that was all I wanted. It became a constant source of conflict, eventually leading to relationship breakdown. The only other thing that calmed my hyper-vigilance was alcohol - a very common form of self-soothing. Van Der Kolk states that you're seven times more likely to be alcoholic if you've suffered childhood trauma.

So, as you can imagine, neither of those methods of calming the hyper-vigilance were healthy - either in a relationship, or out of one. But the overall effect of the hyper-vigilance was that for much of my life, I struggled to be emotionally intimate and connected with any partner. I was physically unable to feel love - either from, or for my partner. For a long time, it felt like my abusive and loveless childhood had condemned me to a life without love.

That wasn't the only way that relationships were difficult though. Another major source of difficulty was what Pete Walker, in his book *'Complex PTSD: from Surviving to Thriving'* (4), called our "inner and outer critics". Walker states that if we've suffered repeated childhood trauma at the hands of our parents or primary caregivers, our reality is completely warped by this. Through our childhood experience we gain core beliefs about the world, other people and ourselves, which become hard-wired into our brains and determine our 'reality'. If we've suffered repeated and ongoing abuse in childhood, we'll have a hard-wired core-belief that the world is an awful, dangerous and scary place, and that no-one can be trusted. Worst of all, we'll believe that we ourselves are intrinsically worthless and bad. If we've been constantly punished for no apparent reason - for no evident wrongdoing, then we come to believe that we must be fundamentally defective and wrong, so we've been punished for just being ourselves. This leads to a deep-seated self-loathing and self-hatred. We continually insult, degrade and demean ourselves. This is the 'inner critic' at work. If we're not doing that, we're instead being critical or angry about all the faults in the world and in other people. That's the 'outer critic' at work. The inevitable end-result of the work of the inner and outer critics is that the people who are most in need of the healing that love can bring - those people most damaged by the total absence of love in their childhood, are the people who can be most difficult to love. Intimate relationships can be the foundation of so much of our joy and happiness in life, but for me they were often the opposite - bringing heartbreak, pain and increased self-loathing, so much so, that one relationship almost killed me - my relationship with Maria.

Maria was wildly beautiful and fiercely intelligent. Our relationship was one of the most significant in my life. It was also one of the shortest. No relationship was ever going to work that had such an imbalance of self-esteem between the partners. Maria was supremely confident and self-assured. I worshipped the very ground she walked on. But I didn't worship myself. I didn't love, or even like myself. I thought I was worthless, nothing - compared to her. It was such a mis-match, the ending was inevitable. She ended the relationship, ending that fantasy I was nurturing of somehow managing to marry the woman of my dreams. But, although she broke my heart, our relationship pushed me towards a life of much greater meaning, purpose and fulfilment. It was my broken heart which gave me the energy and motivation to move in that direction.

Whilst we were together, Maria once said to me: 'You need to get an education - you need to go on an Access course'. Access courses are designed to prepare mature students for university, but I didn't know that at the time. I knew nothing about education, as I'd had so little of it, having 'bunked off' most of my last two years of school, then gone straight into work after that. Thanks to her though, I was going to learn.

After Maria ended the relationship, I spent months in emotional agony. Searching desperately for any little ray of hope, I remembered her advice. That's what I'd do – I'd get an education – I would go on an Access course! My desperate hope was that maybe then I'd be 'good enough' for Maria.

That was an incredibly powerful motivation. I devoted myself to my studies, devouring learning as if my life depended on it. It didn't work though. She didn't want me.

During the college's term-time, I'd had no time to think about anything but college work, but when the college shut down for Christmas, that all changed. I had time to think about my life and feel all the feelings I'd buried during the mad rush of term-time. I realised that my dream was dead. The heartbreak that I'd held slightly in-check, with the idea of becoming good enough for Maria, now hit me with full force. Desperately sad and lonely, one night, I went out and got drunk. Whilst drunk, I made a mistake. I had a one-night stand with someone who was in a relationship. I hated myself for it. I was consumed by self-loathing. That loathing drove me to the top of a mountain in the pouring rain.

I was suicidal. I was sat in my car, rain streaming down the window and tears pouring down my cheeks, sobbing my heart out and planning to kill myself. I found out later, when I trained to be a counsellor, that's the warning sign to watch out for: Although feeling suicidal and thinking suicidal thoughts is awful, it's when people start to make plans for how they're going to actually do it, that it's considered to be a serious danger to life. And that's where I was. I was sat, engine running, my foot revving the pedal, planning to drive my car over the side of the mountain. In that moment, it seemed to be a good plan - to be a really certain way to end the pain.

But something started to faintly call out in the corner of my mind - some faint hint of light found a gap in the pitch-black depths of my depression and despair. I remembered something about the Access course - about what it stood for and did for the students who took the course.

Access courses offer a second chance at education, for people who'd thought that all their chances in life had already come and gone. They offer their students the chance to transform their lives, to have a worthwhile and satisfying career - not just a job - but a career! But more than that, Access courses offer the chance for students to transform their view of *themselves*, offering the possibility that they might actually be worth something more than they currently believe they are. Access courses offer hope.

I remembered that. I remembered one particular day on the course when I was looking around at all the other students, thinking about how much the course had already transformed our view of what might be possible for us in our lives. I remembered looking at the lecturers on the course and thinking: 'That's one hell of a job that you do - to bring transformation and hope to all these people'.

That's what saved my life.

I thought: 'I could do a job like that! If my life isn't worth anything to me, then maybe I could try and make it worth something to other people'.

That's what took my foot off the revs - what stopped me from driving my car over the side of the mountain. I resolved that I would follow the example of the lecturers on my course. I would make that the meaning and purpose of my life, my reason to carry on living - to do a job that in some way made a positive difference to people's lives.

So that's the deal I made with myself. That's what drove the relentless hunger in me for ever-more knowledge and understanding of people, and of the meaning and purpose of life. That's what drove me on in my studies at college, at university, through my postgraduate degree, in my counselling training, and of course, most of all, in my job - the job that saved my life.

I became a college lecturer. That made all the work worthwhile - both the work it took to get the job and the work it took to do it well. Knowing just how transformative the Access course had been for me, made me want to always do my very best for the students I taught. So I worked hard and worked long hours. But it was worth it! Although I still sometimes struggled with life, my struggles now had meaning, with every obstacle overcome bringing fulfilment, a sense of pride and significant achievement. I had discovered and was living according to that truth which Victor Frankl noted in *'Man's Search for Meaning'*: "Those who have a 'why' to live, can bear with almost any 'how'." (5)

This didn't make all my problems go away, but it did make them much easier to bear. If I go to that dark place, what brings me out is the thought of how I might be able to be of some use to others. And I think that's a solution that's open to all of us, not necessarily through changing our jobs, but with just a change of focus on how we live and go about our daily lives, in our everyday interactions and relationships with our colleagues, neighbours, friends, family and community. Research has shown that this is one of the most effective ways to improve our lives - by helping others improve theirs (6).

Living and working with this particular purpose led me to learn some fundamental truths about life. And I began to realise I was strangely fortunate - that I was uniquely positioned to gain so much from my work in this way. As Rhik Samadder notes, in his discussion of childhood trauma and depression, *'I Never Said I Loved You'*: A traumatic childhood damages you and sets you apart from everyone else. It often leaves you in the position of isolated observer, whilst the rest of the world is fully present and immersed in the joys and pleasures of life. But although trauma damages, it also brings unexpected gifts. The experience of trauma can instil a deep compassion and awareness of suffering, along with a unique perspective on the world, which brings an ability to see things that many other people miss (7).

My painful past-history had now yielded a positive pay-off. And I'll try to share some of that bounty with you, as we go to the place where I first reaped that reward: the classroom.

But before we go there, I'd like to leave you with the most important lesson I learned through my life experience - a lesson which has kept me alive and helped build a solid foundation of self-respect and self-belief:

Life can be painful, but it's joyful too. However bad things might seem, I can make it through. I'm not a victim, I'm a survivor. I can change and make it better.

And if that's true for me, then I think it's true for you too:

It will get better. You can make it better.

You can change your life.

Exercise:

Reflect on how you can bring more meaning and purpose into your life:

- How can you, or do you, make a positive difference to those around you – to your family, your friends, at work and in your community?

Chapter 2: The Lesson

Most people would agree that a good teacher or lecturer is someone who's very knowledgeable - an 'expert' in their subject. However, although subject knowledge is essential for successful teaching, I've come to realise that trying to be an 'expert' at developing and maintaining good relationships with my students is far more important.

Ultimately, the job of any teacher or lecturer is to bring out the best in people – to help them realise their potential. That's what teaching is really all about. Think about your favourite teachers or lecturers. They were the ones who made you want to learn, want to work hard - want to do your best. That's why you remember them and not others. So if you have an understanding of its real purpose, doing that job can teach you some fundamental lessons about people and life.

The first lesson I learned as a lecturer, is that to bring out the best in people, you have to create the right conditions for that to happen.

I found that really tough at first.

I was teaching sociology to 16-18 year-old students. It was a subject I was really passionate about. But my passion and enthusiasm for my subject ran into a wall of their complete indifference. They didn't care about government policies and severe inequalities, or any of the other topics in sociology that I thought were important. They cared about their mobile phones, their friends, the funny clips on YouTube and the attractive boys or girls sitting near them in class. But they didn't care about sociology. Not like I did. And that made me really frustrated. I got frustrated when they didn't listen, when they talked instead of working or were on their phones during the lesson. Sometimes this frustration turned to anger - when they ignored me or were rude - when they were being 'bad' students. In my eyes, there were many bad students.

I did have some 'good' students though. The good ones were attentive, diligent and hard-working. I liked them and showed them I did, by giving them lots of praise and encouragement.

Not like the 'bad' ones. I didn't like them. It often seemed like they were my opponents, rather than my students. It felt like they were disrespecting me with their behaviour, wasting my time, making it hard for me to do my job. I tried to address their behaviour in the way I'd been taught to: I told them off when they didn't listen or do what they were asked. I sent them out of class if they kept misbehaving, or at worst, I began the formal disciplinary procedures that could ultimately get them excluded from college. But it never seemed to make any difference. They carried on being 'bad'. And I carried on disliking them.

I was having problems in other areas as well. In addition to teaching sociology, I was also the personal tutor on an Access course, responsible for helping students with anything that was preventing them from being successful in college. As their personal tutor, I was their unofficial counsellor. It seemed that every week I'd have at least one student break down in front of me, telling me they were struggling to feed their kids, or being threatened by an abusive ex-partner, or suffering with anxiety over their ability to handle the demands of the course. Sometimes I'd get three or four students breaking down in front of me and crying hysterically, all in one day. And I couldn't handle it. I really wanted to help them, but I had no idea what to do or how to do it. I didn't have the tools. I was failing, at the job that was so important to me. I had to do better.

Knowing that I needed more skills to do my job successfully, I enrolled on a counselling course. Although it added a full day's work every week to an already-packed schedule, it seemed like the best solution. But I had no idea how incredibly transformative this decision would be.

There's a huge body of knowledge and theory that's been generated over the years to try to deal with the problem of the human condition. However, despite the huge diversity of theories within the fields of counselling and psychotherapy, there is one key, foundational fact that all counsellors and psychotherapists understand:

We are all a product of our experience.

It's not just traumatic experiences like mine which have an impact. We're all shaped by our experiences, *made* into the people we've become by what's happened in our lives - particularly in our childhood. Although we're all born with different genetic potential, whether and how that potential is realised, depends on our upbringing and environment.

This is the focus of almost all work done in therapy – to process and work through the experiences that have caused emotional and behavioural difficulties in life, due to how they've shaped, changed, or damaged us.

Although I learnt many other important and life-changing ideas through my counselling training, this was the big one - the tipping point. This was the new perspective that opened my eyes to see a completely different way of living, being, and relating to people and the world.

Remember those 'bad' students I was talking about – the ones I disliked? It began with them.

If you walk into any staffroom in any school, college or university, you'll hear some teachers talking in the same way about their students, judging and labelling them: talking about how one student is a really good student, that another one was lazy or bad, or another was a waste of time. It sounds unpleasant, but it's unavoidable. It's an integral part of the job. We have to prepare progress reports for our managers, reports for parents' evenings, and references for university applications. These judgements are required. But the problem is that the massive pressure to achieve results, along with the huge and ever-increasing workload that teachers have to deal with, means that sometimes, some students may get 'written off' by teachers, if they seem like a lost cause.

I was no different - just like any other teacher, I made judgements about my students. I also acted on those judgements. So, just like other teachers, with the 'bad' or 'waste of time' students – I didn't waste my time on them.

But then I started counselling training and learnt that lesson - understood that huge idea:

We are all a product of our experience.

And most importantly, I started to apply this understanding to my teaching.

I remember the very moment this change began. I was looking around at my students, for whom I had just set an activity. I noticed one student, who I'll call Rachel, was talking instead of working, as usual. She'd always seemed sullen and resentful, but in that moment, I saw something different in her face – a brief flash of vulnerability. It was the catalyst for a much-needed modification of my perspective. I walked over to her table, and instead of scolding her or standing over her in an intimidating manner, I sat down on my heels in front of her desk, so that we were now at eye-level. I gently enquired *"how are you doing?"* At last, I had become someone to whom she could confess 'I just don't get it'. She wasn't sullen, she was understandably unhappy, feeling 'thick' and victimised. But it was me who'd been thick. I'd been the cause of her unhappiness and inability to learn. I was ashamed. But shame is a great motivator. I vowed to change and look with 'new eyes' at all of my students.

It now became clear that my judgements about my students and the labels and treatment I'd given them were wrong. I now understood that judgements of good or bad were inappropriate, the key issue was a matter of luck:

- There were those students who were lucky enough to have had the kind of upbringing and life experience which had made them the type of hardworking, diligent and attentive students that teachers loved to have in their class.

- Then, there were those who weren't so lucky, who hadn't had all the care and attention they needed, in order for them to value themselves and believe they could succeed.

I realised I had to stop telling off, or writing off, those 'unlucky' students. That didn't mean I became a 'push-over', or tolerated behaviour which disrupted the class; it just meant that I changed how I reacted to it. I now knew that instead of my negative judgements and behaviour, what they actually needed and deserved was much more from me, not less: more of my care, attention, praise and encouragement. We had to be team-mates, instead of opponents. I had to be their chief cheerleader and sup-porter, always on their side. I needed to give them what their upbringing and life so far had not given them, to help them develop some self-worth and self-belief. I had to show them that they were valued, that they were just as good and worthwhile as anyone else in the class.

Luckily though, this was now easy. Knowing that their lives may have been more difficult and less happy than others' made me admire them and really appreciate their achievements. This didn't mean I disliked the other students; I still liked them as much as I had previously, as they were still just as nice as they had always been. What it meant was that I now liked everybody!

Imagine what a difference that makes to life. We all tend to have people in our lives that we dislike, or find it difficult to get on with. Difficult relationships make life difficult. This is particularly true at work. Can you imagine liking all the people who you currently find annoying? Imagine that… just by understanding that those people are not 'bad', but are instead just a product of their experience; you can learn to make all your relationships and therefore all of your life, much health-ier and happier.

My work life was immediately transformed by this new perspective. What made this transformation most apparent was those staffroom con-versations I mentioned earlier. The students to whom I taught sociol-ogy were taught other subjects by other lecturers. I often heard other lecturers talking about the bad students who they'd sent out of class or to the head of school for disciplinary meetings. Very often, those same students were also in my classes, but I was no longer having those problems. I no longer had any bad students.

Their academic performance was also transformed. It had previously been the case that the 'unlucky' students were unlikely to do well in exams. Not anymore. They now tended to achieve much more than they were expected to, rather than less, as had happened too often before. Aided by the excellent work of my colleagues, we took our sociology team, based in one of the most deprived areas in the country, into the top 10% of the UK's educational performance tables.

I didn't know it at the time, but it turned out that I was seeing proof of what Dale Carnegie had said way back in 1936, in one of the highest-selling books of all time; *'How to Win Friends and Influence People'*. Quoting the greatest psychologists and philosophers of his time, he demonstrated that the way to get the best out of people was to abandon condemnation and criticism, because they only ever led to resentment, anger, demoralisation and defensiveness (8).

People get defensive when they feel in some way, attacked and unsafe. Feeling attacked activates the instinctual fight/flight/freeze mode in our brains and deactivates the rational, logical thinking part – the prefrontal cortex. So, telling my students off meant they'd felt 'unsafe' and been incapable of learning, because they literally couldn't think. As the psychologist Abraham Maslow noted, people's basic needs for safety and security have to be met before they can attend to their higher-order needs for learning and self-actualisation (9).

Carnegie stated that to get the best out of people, rather than 'attacking' them, you need to give them what they crave; to be appreciated and to feel good about themselves. When you do this, people always want more of it. As Carnegie noted; we don't just *want* to feel good about ourselves; we *crave* it – it's one of our deepest desires. To satisfy this craving, in order to continue to feel good, people will naturally repeat the behaviour that led to them being praised and appreciated in the first place. In my students' case, this meant that they were no longer feeling defensive or resentful about being told off. They were instead, feeling good, because of the positive attention and the praise for all of their efforts and achievements, which of course only led to even greater levels of effort and achievement.

These huge improvements had mainly come about through applying that all-important lesson from the counselling course. But that wasn't the only thing that had brought these positive changes. There was another piece of foundational knowledge from that training, which naturally followed on from the fact that we're all a product of our experience. This was knowledge of relationship-building, which has been so influential that it now forms the basis of *all* counsellor-client relationships and therapy. This came from the work of one of the most important psychologists of all time - Carl Rogers.

I'd been applying what Rogers (10) called the 'core conditions' for effective counselling and relationship building:

- Unconditional positive regard

- Empathy

- Congruence

But how did this apply to teaching? :

- I had unconditional positive regard for my students: I valued and liked them all unconditionally and made sure they knew it. They didn't have to prove they were good students, as I was now certain they all were - if I just gave them the chance to be.

- I empathised with my students, doing my best to understand them and see the world from their perspective. So, I could understand, that even if their behaviour was in any way 'bad', it didn't mean that *they* were bad - they were just *a product of their experience.*

- I was congruent - genuine with my students, so that they could clearly see and believe that I valued and respected them.

Rogers applied these ideas for many years in his work as a therapist. They were also rigorously tested in his research.

Rogers fundamentally believed that we were all, essentially, good people. It was only the effects of bad childhood experiences that caused problems in our behaviour- that caused us to stop being our 'real' selves. He believed that everyone who was in therapy was just struggling with the problem of trying to become the person they should really be - that they were born to be. Rogers found, through his work in research and with his clients, that if the 'core conditions' mentioned above were applied in therapy, clients would move to become much more genuine, confident and happy with themselves. He found this to be true, even with the most extreme cases, such as prisoners who'd been convicted of terrible crimes. Rogers found that even these clients, when receiving the core conditions, moved towards a much more positive place in themselves - they began to become better people. It might take much longer with them, due to the damaging past experiences which had led to them ending up in jail. But eventually, when given unconditional positive regard and empathy, even those who are so often considered the worst and unredeemable, become better people. And this was proved in Rogers' research. Proved - scientifically tested and found to be true.

Pretty astounding, isn't it? Quite simply, Rogers' research showed that if you treat people like good people, they will *be* good people. It's worth remembering that - isn't it?

If you treat people like good people, they will *be* good people.

It feels like a useful motto for life. Particularly as it's been tested and proved. And applying it to my work confirmed its value. Rogers' ideas brought out the best in me and helped me do the same for my students.

Being the best that we can be is the ultimate goal of life. That's why these ideas have become key guiding principles.

You can change your life

We are all a product of our experience

If you treat people like good people, they will *be* good people

---

Exercise: Reflect on your personal experience as a child and the challenges it presented:

- What messages did you receive regarding what it was possible for you to do or be and achieve in life?

- In what ways might these messages have shaped your life?

---

strugling
with The challenge
of being ourselves
becoming
Carl Rogers

Chapter 3: You are a Hero

I was ten years old when I first watched 'Star Wars'. I queued for over an hour to see it. At that time, the cinemas in my home town only had one screen, so when a blockbuster like Star Wars was on, you knew that you were going to have to queue if you wanted to see it. Star Wars was so worth the wait though. It was the best film I'd ever seen. And at the end, the whole cinema audience stood up and clapped and cheered. It was amazing!

After that, all I wanted to be was a Jedi Knight. That was my childhood dream. But it seems that it's not just children who have those dreams. Information obtained from the last two government Census surveys in the UK revealed that hundreds of thousands of people in the UK claimed that their religion was 'Jedi Knight'. Not something you'd expect an adult would put in an official government survey, is it?

You have a lot in common with those 'Jedi Knights' though. Actually, to be more precise, you have a lot in common with Luke Skywalker - the Jedi Knight hero of the Star Wars films. Yes really - you do! I do too. We all do. On our individual life- journeys, our stories mirror his, and in their own way are all equally 'heroic'.

This was something that I discovered one night in the most unexpected way, through going to a dance class. Dancing - not usually the time when you expect to learn great lessons in life. But this wasn't your usual run-of-the-mill dancing though. This wasn't the normal 'step to the side, step to the other side' stuff you see at most parties or nightclubs. This stuff was crazy! At times it was difficult to even call it dancing. I'd never seen anything like it. But what was especially strange, was that no-one seemed remotely bothered by the dancers' crazy antics. No-one was batting an eyelid. It felt like I'd stepped through a door into an alternate universe where all the normal rules of human conduct had been revoked. But despite the similarities, I wasn't 'in a galaxy far, far away'. This was real life, in a church hall in Cardiff, Wales. There was nothing other-worldly about it, just a wooden dance-floor, dimmed lights and a DJ. The dancing wasn't alcohol or drug-fuelled either. Everyone was straight and sober, but on the natural high of the weird and wonderful world of 5Rhythms.

5Rhythms, where, to use the immortal line from *'Grease'*, 'The rules is there ain't no rules'. 5Rhythms is where people go to *really* dance.

I love dancing, but I've struggled to find anywhere to dance that I like enough. In clubs and bars, you can't really dance. Yes, I know, people are dancing, but, it's always dancing on their best behaviour - meaning they're dancing according to the 'rules'. You didn't know that there are rules to dancing, did you? But there are. You may not be consciously aware of these rules, but you almost definitely follow them. And if you watch closely, you can start to see what they are.

There are countless social rules which we all follow all of the time, without realising it. There are rules for eating, talking, walking, sitting; unwritten rules for every kind of behaviour, for every social situation, including dancing.

Next time that you go to any social event where people are dancing, watch what they're doing. They're always doing the socially accepted dance-moves, like the old 'step to the side, step to the other side' routine you always see. That's something that I've always had a problem with. When you love a song or dance track and feel that you absolutely *have to* get up and dance to it; at that point, the old 'step to the side' routine just doesn't cut it. When you love the music that much, then you really want to cut loose and dance in a way that reflects how much it moves you, don't you? I know I do. But the problem is that even though we might feel that way, we don't actually do it. Because it's not 'allowed'. Because it doesn't follow the 'rules'. Because people would look at us, people would stare, judge us and make us feel that we were weird and 'wrong'. That's the big problem, the thing that we are all scared of - being judged. In fact, some people are so worried about being judged in this way that they never get up and dance at all. They never get to let their hair down and just be themselves. And because we're *all* so scared of being judged, none of us get to really be ourselves. We never get to find out who we really are, what we're really like, what we might be capable of, if we weren't subject to this social judging that happens all the time - not just when dancing, but in all aspects of life.

The fear of judgement weighs us down, chains and constrains us. It stops us being or becoming who we really are, being all that we can be.

But, by going to a 5Rhythms dance class, I was able to see what's possible when we're no longer living in fear of being judged. At 5Rhythms, there are no steps to learn or rules to follow; you just go and 'dance like no-one is watching'. It's a workout, a meditation, an expression and release of energy. It's group therapy and the best night's clubbing you've ever had (11).

It was a revelation to me; like a circus of human freedom. I saw a rave, a mosh-pit and graceful ballet, every kind of creative expression. There was running, jumping, spinning and twisting, and writhing around on the floor. There was whooping and hollering, screaming and laughing; there were adults freely at play. I saw people at peace - with each other and themselves. People were smiling - at each other and to themselves. I saw joy.

The class was a journey through the five rhythms: rhythms matched with the energies, moods, phases and patterns of life. It moved from gentle flowing music and movement, through wild, chaotic dancing and ending in 'stillness'. That night, despite the energy of the session, it was the stillness that moved me most.

During the session, I'd really thrown myself into the dancing. I had totally let myself go, particularly during the energetic 'staccato' and 'chaos' rhythm sections. I guess I must've had a lot on my mind that I needed to get out of my system. Towards the end, as the music and dancing wound down into 'stillness', I remember lying on the floor, motionless, without a single thought crossing my mind. I'd never felt so relaxed. But although relaxed and still, I felt full of life. I felt like the 'old me' was gone. All the old cares, worries and insecurities that had filled my mind and weighed me down had vanished. I felt purged. Cleansed. I felt transformed, like a new person. I lay on the floor, listening to my heart and experiencing the blood pumping through my veins, aware of nothing but the feeling of being alive - truly alive.

Later that night, reflecting in bed, I realised why it had felt so therapeutic. 5Rhythms had done what all therapy seeks to do. It took me on a transformational journey. It helped me to 'shed the skin' of my old life, my old ways of thinking, feeling and being - even if only for one night. And I realised what had made this journey possible – it was acceptance. At 5Rhythms, you're treated as a good person, as 'good enough', exactly as you are. The person you are is perfectly acceptable and accepted and so, therefore, is everything you do. The research into the therapeutic effects of 5Rhythms confirms this (12): It's that lack of judgement which enables everyone to 'dance like no-one is watching', to lose themselves and feel free to really be themselves. And reflecting on these liberating and empowering effects made me realise; this acceptance was what Carl Rogers referred to as 'unconditional positive regard'.

Making that connection was the 'Eureka!' moment which made everything clear. I saw that once again, Rogers was right. Receiving unconditional positive regard from the other dancers enabled me to 'let myself go', be 'transformed' and feel like a 'new person'. And taking that journey meant I'd been doing what Rogers said we're all doing - struggling with the challenge of becoming ourselves.

Rogers stated that we all grow up living according to the 'conditions of worth' laid down by our parents. This means that we grow up being constantly subject to their judgement. We're generally only shown love and appreciation by our parents if we meet their conditions - if we live according to their values and worldview. This results in us taking on and living according to a set of values, ideas and rules which often don't match up with who we really are, meaning we're not being our true selves. So, for example, we may grow up living according to the ideas that boys should be tough, not sensitive, or girls should be dainty and pretty, not strong. Or, we may grow up being made to feel we're stupid or useless and that we should never try to achieve anything, that we're not worthy of success. These ideas will shape our lives. They'll shape our thinking and guide our behaviour because we'll always be unconsciously feeling that we're only okay, good enough or safe if we conform to these rules and ideas.

It's living according to these conditions of worth and the struggle to overcome them that causes us to experience emotional difficulties. Rogers stated that we all strive in this way and that the way to approach these problems was essentially to shed the skin of our old selves - just like a snake, so as to become the next best version of ourselves. We have to throw off the chains of the old conditions of worth laid down by our parents and become free to be who we really are, by living according to the values, rules and ideas we've developed for ourselves.

Rogers stated that the reason we struggle this way is because we all have the potential and power within us to become free to be who we're meant to be. That's what causes us to struggle against the conditions of worth which constrain us. Rogers called this built-in power and potential the 'self-actualising tendency'.

Self-actualisation is a concept made famous by the psychologist Abraham Maslow. For Maslow, self-actualisation referred to the final stage of human development, the fulfilment of one's potential (13). Carl Rogers believed that the key driver and motivation behind *all* human behaviour was the self-actualising tendency - the drive to fulfil our potential.

This is a view that was shared by arguably the most important philosopher of the nineteenth century, Friedrich Nietzsche. Nietzsche was insistent on the 'will to power' being the driving force behind all life. This primal force is our instinctive, intrinsic urge to grow, be more and better. It's the psychological drive to achieve our higher self through mastering or overcoming our current self (14). Rogers, Maslow and Nietzsche are all describing the same thing - the same primary drive and motivation in all human beings - to fulfil our potential and be the best and all that we can be.

The will to power, or self-actualising tendency, drives all of us to try and shed the skin of our old lives and old selves. This is why so many stories, books and films discuss and describe the struggle or the journey to 'find ourselves'. It's the reason so many people travel; go on pilgrimages and spiritual retreats - to find themselves. It's why people go to 5Rhythms. We're *all* on life's journey, seeking to find ourselves, self-actualise and become our true self.

And this isn't a recent fad - a product of our modern, self-centred society. This understanding of life as a journey to find ourselves is something that's documented in all the great myths, legends and stories of all the great societies throughout human history.

This is clearly shown in the much-celebrated work of Joseph Campbell, '*The Hero with a Thousand Faces*' (15). In this book, Campbell shows how the great myths and legends that have documented and inspired human history follow the same pattern or storyline: The hero hears or receives a 'call to adventure' and then sets out on a quest, leaving their old life behind. They struggle with powerful forces, then return home as a hero, having fulfilled their destiny - to become the person they were always meant to be. The hero returns with treasure. The treasure represents some fundamental quality or wisdom that saved or transformed their lives, which is of great worth to their society. The book describes how all of the great stories which are designed to guide us in our lives follow this same pattern, particularly the stories of the lives of the Buddha, Mohammed and Jesus; all of whose stories followed this pattern of 'the Hero's Journey'.

Campbell's work draws on the many rites of passage found in so many societies throughout the world in which a person is required to leave their old life and identity behind and undergo a difficult trial or test. Passing that test brings the reward of full acceptance into their tribe or society. They can then take their place as a new person, the person that they were born to be - the fully-developed adult citizen their tribe or society needs.

And crucially, Campbell's work draws on the psychological theories of Sigmund Freud and Carl Jung, to demonstrate how all the great stories and myths reflect the personal psychological journeys we all take. Campbell stated how the common themes that run throughout the great myths, legends and stories are clearly designed to help us win through on the 'heroic journey of our own lives'.

Campbell's work, Nietzsche's philosophy, Maslow's and Rogers' theories confirm this fundamental truth about human life: we're all on our own personal Hero's Journey – to become the person we are meant to be.

That's why the big action and adventure blockbusters we see at the cinema make such exciting and compulsive viewing - because they follow that same pattern and story-structure. *The Lord of the Rings*; *The Hunger Games*; *The Wizard of Oz*; *Mulan*; *Harry Potter*; *Rocky* - these are just a few examples of movies which feature the Hero's Journey.

That's why people like those in the UK Government Census identify with and as 'Jedi Knights'. When George Lucas was writing *Star Wars*, he consciously followed the template and pattern of the Hero's Journey he'd read about in Joseph Campbell's book. Luke Skywalker's journey is the Hero's Journey. He receives a 'call to adventure' and leaves his old life and identity behind. He battles against dark forces, finally winning through when he achieves his destiny of becoming his true, or real self, what he was born to be - a Jedi Knight.

Therefore, Luke Skywalker's story is essentially all of our stories - the stories of our own personal Hero's Journey to self-actualise. And so 'The

Force', which Luke Skywalker draws on in order to complete his journey, can be seen as the force which is in us and drives us all; the self-actualising tendency; the built-in power and potential to be all that we can be.

So it's your story.

You're on a journey and are being called to adventure- called to break free from your conditions of worth and find out who you really are and could be. The treasure you'll find if you seek it out is the better version of yourself, a person you can be proud of, who you were born to be. This is your task, your mission and duty. With great power comes great responsibility. You are called to use your power to make life better for you and everyone around you.

We all possess this power, to help both ourselves and others become the best that we all can be.

As Rogers' research showed: It's unconditional positive regard and empathy which enables people to self-actualise; it's acceptance – as seen at 5Rhythms. It's understanding that we're all a product of our experience. It means if you treat people like good people, they will *be* good people.

You don't need to be a Jedi Knight to do this, or a counsellor, a teacher, lecturer, or even a dancer. Everyone can do it.

You have the power.

You can be the hero of your own life and the hero that others may need in theirs.

May The Force be with you! ☺

You can change your life

We are all a product of our experience

If you treat people like good people, they will _be_ good people

We are all on a journey

Exercise:

Try to notice the difference in people when you provide the core conditions of unconditional positive regard, empathy and congruence in your relationship with them

---

Chapter 4: Change what you do, to Change You

The 2005 film *'Batman Begins'* is another example of the Hero's Journey. In this film, Bruce Wayne, played by Christian Bale, leaves his pampered billionaire lifestyle behind, in order to understand the criminal mind and so more effectively fight criminals. His travels take him into many different adventures, during which he truly loses himself - he ends up in a prison in Asia. He's rescued by a man who becomes his mentor (another common theme in the Hero's Journey). His mentor helps him in the final stage of his journey to lose his old self - his old fears and insecurities. Bruce Wayne is then taught all the skills he needs to return home and fulfil his destiny of becoming his new, better self - Batman.

At a crucial point in this film, Christian Bale's character states, *"it's not who I am underneath, but what I do that defines me"*. This may surprise you, but Batman's words contain within them a wisdom which is truly life-changing.

However, before we go any further, I think it's important to acknowledge that changing your life; to start thinking and behaving in the way I am encouraging you to do, may not feel entirely easy or natural to you. You may have read up to this point and thought something like: *'That all sounds great, but I'm just not that kind of person - I can't help feelings of frustration getting in the way of seeing the best in people. Why should I bother?'*

I understand that feeling. I've often read books which left me feeling really fired up! I'd be inspired by new amazing ideas which promised to change my life and change the world, bringing me a euphoric sense of hope and optimism. But all too often, that initial optimism faded and normal life resumed, leaving me feeling frustrated, disappointed and hopeless - that my life would never change.

But then, I started training to be a counsellor, and this training revealed to me what I'd been doing wrong - why those great ideas had never brought any lasting improvements: I hadn't applied them to my life - I hadn't put them into *practice*.

I needed to train myself in these new ways of thinking and behaving. I needed to make them habitual - my automatic ways of being.

On the counselling course, we practiced putting the 'core conditions' of unconditional positive regard, empathy and congruence into action, in the simulated counselling sessions that we had with each other. At first, this was difficult - it felt unnatural, and we often got it wrong. But eventually, it became much easier ; it became automatic. Looking back on our progress as trainee counsellors, it was incredible to see how much we'd all progressed. And this progression was just a simple matter of practice.

So, having learnt and practiced applying the core conditions on the counselling course, I then began to apply them at work, in my relationships with my students. And once again, this didn't feel natural at first, as it contradicted so much of what I'd previously been taught to do as a lecturer. But once again, with practice, this new way of thinking and behaving became automatic.

And so it became clear to me that on our own individual Hero's Journey, if we want to fulfil our destiny and self-actualise, we need to follow Batman's example and train ourselves through our actions to become the people we want to be.

"It's not who I am underneath, but what I do that defines me". We may not 'naturally' be the kind of person who is empathetic and non-judgemental, who can follow the advice of 'if you treat people like good people, they will *be* good people'. But if we start to practice being this kind of person, then we'll *become* this kind of person. That's why Batman's line is so important; because it contains a real truth.

You are defined by what you do, because **changing the way we behave, changes us**. Therefore, if we want to become a different and better person, we can become that person by training ourselves to be different and better.

Aristotle, the legendary Greek philosopher, said that virtues are ways of being that we have made a habit - we become virtuous by performing virtuous acts, which we have decided to do, in order to learn to be virtuous (16).

And although this is truly 'ancient' wisdom, it is backed up by contemporary scientific research. A crucially important finding of modern neuroscience is that the brain is malleable - it can change and grow. *You* can change and grow. You're not stuck in the mould you were born into. Although we're all a product of our experience, we can deliberately have new experiences that can re-shape who we are (17).

As David Brooks explains in his book '*The Social Animal*'; neurons (brain cells) are connected by synapses. These connections, or synapses, are what the brain creates to store information. The brain works through creating networks of stored information, networks of connected brain cells and synapses that help us to process information and understand the world. When we begin to learn something new, we start to create a new network in our brain. The more a new activity is done, the more the network is increased in size and strength. Therefore, if we deliberately practice a new way of behaving, that way of behaving will become hardwired into our new neural network, which then becomes our new way of being. So, although at first, the new activity, new skill, or new way of behaving may be difficult, it will eventually become second nature. For example, consider how difficult and scary it was when you first sat behind the wheel of a car; all those things that you had to try and remember to do, all at the same time - it felt impossible! But, through constant practice, you became 'expert', so much so, that you no longer have to think about it when you drive - it happens almost automatically.

This is because the human brain works by turning conscious knowledge into unconscious knowledge so that actions become automatic, like driving, which frees up the brain to actively concentrate on other things. It is the process of turning something new, which requires concentration, into a habit - an automatic behaviour - which requires no concentration (18).

Therefore, although you may not yet feel able to be accepting and empathetic, if you deliberately practice doing these things, before long, they'll become automatic.

As Timothy Wilson, Professor of Psychology at the University of Virginia shows: "We are what we do", stating that if we begin to change our behaviour, it begins a cycle of positive reinforcement, whereby the first act of more moral behaviour makes us feel more moral, which then leads to further acts of moral behaviour (19).

This is exactly what Dale Carnegie was saying, in terms of praising and encouraging people in order to get the best out of them. In this case, we are praising and encouraging ourselves for our better behaviour in order to continue to improve and get the best out of ourselves. Therefore, to become a better person, we first have to start acting like one. Every time we act like the better person we wish to be, we'll feel good about ourselves. In order to continue feeling good, we'll naturally repeat the 'better' behaviour which made us feel good in the first place. So by practicing being the person we want to be, we *become* that person.

Or, more simply, as Alcoholics Anonymous put it, you just have to "fake it till you make it".

So please, don't be discouraged by the thought that you're 'not that kind of person' who can think and act in the ways I am suggesting. Whilst you may not be now, you can be, with practice.

This doesn't mean that you're ever going to be perfect, or even that you should try to be; it just means that you can be better than you were. Perfection is not only impossible; aiming for it and believing that's what we should be, is damaging and unhelpful. Just as Jordan Peterson shows in *'12 Rules for Life'*, we shouldn't compare ourselves with other people, those who we might think of as 'perfect'. That can just lead to discouragement, dejection and abandoning our goal of self-improvement, as we may think that we can never be as 'good' as them. But the truth is that we don't need to be as good as anyone else. The only meaningful and necessary comparison is with ourselves. All we need to do is compare ourselves with the person we were yesterday. That's all that matters - that we are, every day, striving to be just a little bit better than we were before.

However, even if we were to compare ourselves to someone who we felt was perfectly able to be accepting, empathetic and non-judgemental, we'd find, if we looked closely, that they only became that way through practice. For example, his Holiness, the 14th Dalai Lama, the spiritual leader of the Tibetan people, maintains his beliefs and his ways of thinking and being through practice. He trains himself through daily meditation on Buddhist principles and beliefs of kindness and compassion. Even the Dalai Lama, who, according to Buddhist belief, was *born* holy - the reincarnation of the previous Dalai Lama; he maintains this holy state through practice (20). But we don't have to attain the same level of holiness or 'perfection' as the Dalai Lama; we just need to try and be a little better than we were yesterday.

So, here's how you get to follow in Batman's footsteps and become the Superhero of your own life. Here's how you win through on your quest to self-actualise and become that person you want to be.

We all know that we're not born being good at anything. We learn to talk, learn to walk, learn to read and write through practice. And in our adult lives, the jobs we do and the careers we develop come about through education and training. The great musicians, artists and athletes who we love to hear and watch, all became great through practice.

So in the same way, you can change your life and be the person you want to be. You can self-actualise and help others do the same.

You can do all this, because **changing the way we behave, changes us.**

What are you waiting for?

You can change your life

We are all a product of our experience

If you treat people like good people, they will *be* good people

We are all on a journey

Changing the way we behave, changes us

<u>Exercise:</u>

Reflect on two interactions you've had with people during your day or week - one that went well and one that was less successful.

For each interaction, consider:

- What the other person said or did – either pleasant or unpleasant/difficult
- How you reacted – either positively or negatively
- What was the outcome of this?
- What could have been different? – How could this have turned out better or worse?

When doing this, it's important to be kind to yourself. Don't get upset if you haven't always managed to think, behave and react in the ways that you wish to. Just by reflecting and reminding yourself of these new ways of thinking and being, you'll be continually making them more a part of yourself. So, even if progress isn't always fast as you would like, don't worry or criticise yourself. Eventually, this repetition of ideas will mean that you'll no longer have to consciously try and think that way- it will become automatic.

Chapter 5: Listen Up!

You may've noticed that all the ideas I've discussed so far have been concerned with changing how we think and behave in all the relationships in our lives. In a book which proposes to reveal answers to life, this focus on relationships may seem a little blinkered, or short-sighted. However, I would argue that this captures the essence of what it means to be human; because human life is all and entirely based around relationships.

And I'm not alone in this view; to quote our friend Aristotle, *"Man is a social animal"*, meaning that the fundamental nature of human beings is to be with other human beings. And from a more contemporary source, Petruska Clarkson's highly acclaimed book *'The Therapeutic Relationship'* focuses entirely on the forms and uses of the relationship in all types of counselling and psychotherapy. She justifies this focus by explaining that to be human, means to be in relationships. She states that it's in relationships that we spend our lives and find the meaning of our lives. All aspects and stages of our lives happen in and through relationships - with our parents, siblings, friends, peers, teachers, co-workers and spouses. It's relationships that make us who we are, just as it's problems in relationships which bring us to counselling or psychotherapy (21).

We're all a product of our experience - our experience in relationships.

Therefore, as every aspect of our lives is spent in relationships, if we improve our relationships, we improve every aspect of our lives.

Carl Rogers became famous for his focus on the relationship between counsellor and client. His approach to relationship building has become so influential that it now forms the basis of all counselling and psychotherapy work. Despite the many different schools of thought within these fields, if you train to be a counsellor, your initial training will consist of learning to use Rogers' approach to relationship building, applying the 'core conditions'. But what makes Rogers' approach to therapy unique is that instead of using the counsellor-client relationship as the basis for various counselling techniques to be applied to the client, in Rogers' approach, **the relationship *is* the therapy**.

Rogers believed that just as a plant will flourish and grow if you create the right conditions, by providing sunlight and water, in the same way, humans will flourish and grow if you provide the 'core conditions' of unconditional positive regard, empathy and congruence.

This is what his experience and research proved. Providing the core conditions in a relationship enables people to realise their potential, self-actualise and become the person they're supposed to be; their real - or true self. And Rogers stated that this kind of relationship is mutually beneficial, bringing psychological growth and wellbeing to each person in the relationship.

And one of the most effective ways to practice providing the core conditions of unconditional positive regard and empathy is to try to use active listening skills in all of your conversations.

Active listening is the first and arguably, most important skill that counsellors learn. This may surprise you, because after all, listening is an ability that most of us are born with - something we do all the time, without thinking about it. Active listening, however, is definitely *not* a skill we're born with. Active listening is so rare and so powerful, that I've seen people break down and cry when they were actively listened to, because they'd never experienced anything like it before.

The reason it's so powerful is because active listening makes people feel valued; makes them feel *seen* - instead of 'invisible' and worthless. It makes them feel that they *matter*. Some people live their whole lives without this experience. And as Dale Carnegie stated, feeling good about ourselves is one of our deepest desires and needs. Active listening fulfils this need.

Active listening means giving your 100% total attention to someone. It means totally focusing on them, on what they are saying and feeling, without interrupting or taking over the conversation - just giving them the chance, permission and encouragement to express how they feel. This makes them feel good, because it shows that what they feel matters to us - that *they* matter to us.

Active listening requires us to not only listen with our total attention; it also requires us to maintain eye contact with the person who's talking, so that they can clearly see that we're with them - that they matter to us and that we're on their side. Whilst maintaining eye contact, we can also show them that we're totally focused on and understand what they're saying, through non-verbal communication, such as nodding our head in agreement or understanding. We may also occasionally sum up or paraphrase what they're saying, so as to show that we listened, we understand and accept them. Whilst maintaining eye contact, we can also more easily see, sense and feel their feelings and emotions. By totally focusing on them and maintaining eye contact in this way, we're then able to empathise with them - to in some way be able to feel what they are feeling. By doing this, we can begin to enter into their world - to see the world as they do - to 'see the world through their eyes'. When we're able to empathise and understand in this way, we're once again able to discard our initial judgements about them, because we can now see how their actions make sense in *their* world. And, most importantly, when they can see that we still accept and value them, and we're not judging them for what they've said, they may then start to accept and value *themselves*.

Is there any better gift you can give to another human being?

And this is something that you can start to practice right now, in all your conversations, in all your relationships. Go and try it, right now. You'll be amazed at what happens.

You'll find that when you actively listen and give people your 100%, undivided attention, people start to open up and talk to you as they've never done before. You're going to find out things that will surprise and amaze you about the people you thought you knew. People you may've thought were dull and ordinary will have the most interesting stories - stories that were there all the time, just waiting for someone to pay attention and really listen to them. So active listening is also a gift to you, because it'll enable you to see and appreciate the value in everyone around you. You'll find that when you actively listen, people will start to come alive and really bloom in front of your eyes, when you give them this gift of your total attention. They'll begin to flourish and grow, because you've provided the right conditions - the core conditions of unconditional positive regard and empathy.

I first saw these powerful effects of active listening in the counselling room with my clients. Through active listening, I was able to connect with my clients, build trust, and develop the all-important relationship between us, which would be the basis of the therapy. That's when I first saw the incredible results of active listening; results which, at the time, I found hard to believe and which are equally hard to explain.

One particular example of this always sticks out in my mind: one of my clients came into a session in more distress than anyone I'd ever seen. He was absolutely despising himself for something he thought he'd done to one of his family. He was hurting so much that I was at a total loss about how to deal with the situation. I had no idea how to help him. I remember thinking to myself, *'I don't think that I can do this job; I don't have the skills to handle situations like this'*. All I could think of doing was to listen - to very actively listen and be 100% present with him and for him. So that's what I did. I was accepting of him and his pain. I empathised and showed that I understood by occasionally paraphrasing back to him what he'd just told me: Paraphrasing so as to not only demonstrate that he'd been heard; but also to help him to clarify what he was feeling and why. At the time, I didn't feel I was doing anything remotely significant or helpful. It didn't feel in any way adequate to deal with the situation. He cried so much that it seemed his pain would never end. But then, around five minutes before the end of the session, he started laughing. He was laughing, whilst wiping away the last of his tears, in relief at unburdening himself and realising he wasn't the evil person he'd thought himself to be. And when he stopped laughing, he was calm, smiling and peaceful. He'd come into the session in more pain than I'd ever witnessed, but then fifty minutes later, he was smiling and laughing. I couldn't explain it. I didn't 'do' anything. I just listened - very actively and carefully listened.

The client I found most challenging to help had been diagnosed with schizophrenia. He'd previously been in hospital due to this issue. When we first met, it was incredibly difficult. Communication was almost non-existent. I found it hard to get a word or any response at all from him. When he did talk, it was really quiet and difficult to hear, and he rarely made eye-contact with me. Week after week we met and week after week, it was difficult. I spoke to my manager a number of times about my concerns - worried that I couldn't help my client. My manager listened and each time told me the same thing: *"just trust the process"*. So that's what I did - I trusted the 'process'; I actively listened. That's the key part of the process. I did my best to encourage my client to talk and very actively listened when he did. By the tenth week of his counselling, my client had started smiling. He'd smile as he came in the door and saw me and smile when he spoke to me. He was relaxed and even told me a couple of jokes. He laughed. He talked to me and looked me in the eyes whilst talking. And he was very visibly a different person - very different from the one who'd come in ten weeks before. He was calm, more confident, relaxed, happy and content. And all I did was listen - actively listen, because I didn't know what else to do. I just trusted in 'the process' - the process of providing the core conditions in the relationship, through active listening. And each time I did that - even with this client I thought I couldn't help - the process worked. Each time, just as Carl Rogers described, the client moved to a more positive place in themselves. When I think back and remember those incidents, the only way I can think of to describe what happened was that it felt miraculous. I'm not religious, but that's what it felt like, because it felt like I hadn't done anything - I just listened. And just through actively listening, something 'miraculous' occurred.

One possible explanation for these astounding effects came from a film I watched about a psychiatrist who was himself struggling with life. The film was called *'Hector and the Search for Happiness'*. Although it was a comedy, it still had some wisdom to offer. When the psychiatrist, feeling like a fraud and that he was useless in his life and work proclaimed that 'all I do is listen', he was offered this comforting advice: *"Listening is loving"*. And maybe there's something in that. To love means to value and appreciate. And when people are valued and appreciated, miraculous things can occur. I don't mean divine intervention, but that people are incredible and awesome. Amazing things can happen when they begin to realise their worth. That's the magic that makes the process work.

The process worked - on the counselling course and now in the counselling room. All the practice had paid off. And because I could see how powerful it was, I started doing it all the time, in all my relationships. And all my relationships improved because of this, most noticeably at work.

I practiced active listening in all conversations with my students, which enabled me to connect and develop a good relationship with them and provide the core conditions in those relationships. I was now able to have much more meaningful conversations with them, which made it much more likely that they'd open up to me if they were anxious, stressed or depressed. I was therefore much more able to provide or organise the support they needed. This improvement became really apparent at the end of my first year of counselling training when I was talking to three of my Access students, who'd all had a really difficult time in college. One had a son who'd suddenly become very ill; another had problems with her partner and also struggled with anxiety over whether she had the time and ability to succeed on the course; the last had issues with dyslexia, which made her feel unintelligent and incapable of succeeding at anything, due to how badly this issue had been dealt with at school. All three had come very close to dropping out of college due to these problems. But despite these issues, all three successfully completed the course. I spoke to them at the end of the last term, at a little celebratory event we organised for our graduating students. Hoping to hear of useful strategies I could pass on to other students, I asked them what had made it possible for them to stay on the course and be as successful as they'd been. To my surprise, in unison, they turned round to me and said *"you did"*. But, once again, I hadn't 'done' anything – I'd just actively listened.

Active listening made me much more successful at work and much happier too, as it improved all of my relationships - with my students, colleagues and with every person I met. Through active listening, I was able to provide the core conditions in my relationships, which therefore improved my relationships, both in and out of work, significantly improving my whole life. But, the crucial point here is not that active listening improved my life; it can improve *your* life too. It can also help to improve the lives of everyone you meet.

As Carl Rogers proved in his research, when you provide the core conditions in a relationship, it becomes therapeutic, as people in these kinds of relationships will begin to move towards a more positive place in themselves. This is because when you've clearly demonstrated that you accept and value them exactly as they are, they can then start to accept and value themselves. This leads to them beginning to believe in their own worth and living according to their own values, rather than living according to the 'conditions of worth' laid down by their parents or primary caregivers. That means they're beginning to become themselves - the person that they're meant to be, rather than who their parents and life experiences had previously made them be. It means they're beginning to self-actualise. And you can help to make this happen, with everyone you meet, in every one of your relationships, in every part of your life, just by active listening. Because, at its heart, active listening is much more than just a skill; it's an understanding that everyone is valuable and worthwhile, if we can just give them the chance to be. It reflects a philosophy which we can apply to all our relationships and all of our lives.

You can do this. You can become a force for good amongst your family and friends, the one who lifts them up when they're down, who they can rely on when they're troubled. You can be a positive force at work, bringing care, affection and support when stress and pressure are taking their toll. You can be the one who holds your family, friends and work-mates together, their rock and foundation stone. You can be the one who makes the difference.

You can start to actively listen in all your conversations, giving people your full and total attention. You can show them that what they think and feel matters - that *they* matter. You can show that you accept and value them exactly as they are, helping them to accept and value themselves. You can help them to begin to self-actualise. You can have a hand in making the miraculous happen.

And now you know that you *can* do this, why wouldn't you - all of the time?

You can change your life

We are all a product of our experience

If you treat people like good people, they will *be* good people

We are all on a journey

Changing the way we behave, changes us

The relationship is the therapy

Exercise:

Practise active listening in all of your conversations

Chapter 6: Connection - for Life!

We're all a product of our experience in relationships. The quality of our relationships determines the quality of our lives. That alone gives us ample reason and motivation to do all we can to prioritise and improve them. But it's more than just our happiness which is determined by our relationships, as the story below shows:

Way back in the 13th century, in Rome, the Holy Roman Emperor, Frederick II, ordered an incredible experiment to be carried out with a group of newborn babies. He wished to discover what language was naturally spoken by babies - to discover what the natural 'inborn' language of humans was. He wished to know whether they would naturally speak what was then thought of as the 'first' human language - Hebrew. This was to be tested by instructing the foster-mothers and nurses of the chosen group of children not to do anything with the children except wash and feed them. There was to be none of the usual talk, play or interaction that would normally be seen between babies and those who cared for them. This would ensure that there was no possibility of the babies being 'contaminated' by hearing their carers' language.

However, he never got to find out whether Hebrew was the natural language of humans, because all of the babies died without saying a word.

Many years later, in the early 1900s, this tragic experiment was unwittingly repeated with orphaned children who were being brought up in institutional care homes. At this time, it was thought that human contact with the children should be kept to a minimum, for the sake of the children's health, so as to promote hygiene and therefore prevent the possibility of infection. Once again, the babies were properly fed, bathed and clothed, but they received no other physical contact or interaction. Once again, the babies died.

The babies died when they contracted the infections that the 'hygienic' conditions were supposed to protect them from. The most 'hygienic' care homes that most stringently followed the rules around avoiding human contact; these had the highest death rates. According to our understanding of how germs cause disease, hygienic conditions should have protected the babies - so what was it that went so tragically wrong?

These deaths were investigated by the psychoanalyst René Spitz. The clear conclusion Spitz drew from his investigation was that, just as with the babies in 13th Century Rome, it was the lack of human interaction and connection which killed these children. It was the absence of these which made the babies incredibly vulnerable to illness and disease. In both cases, the children were properly fed, washed and clothed, with a roof over their heads. All their material physical needs were met. But in both cases, the children died. (22).

Incredible, isn't it? It's unbelievably tragic, but incredible nonetheless. It's astounding that what seems like a purely emotional need is actually crucial for babies' survival. But, what's equally astounding is that it's not just babies who need these things.

In his book *'Lost Connections'*, which focuses on all the essential areas of life which we need to re-connect to, Johann Hari (23) also shows how interaction and connection with other people are vital, but not just for babies - for *everyone*.

Hari explains the key findings of research into loneliness, focusing on the work of John Cacioppo, a researcher in social neuroscience. Cacioppo was interested in cortisol (the hormone produced by stress) and how it might demonstrate the physical impact of loneliness. By measuring the levels of cortisol in people who experienced loneliness, Cacioppo was able to see a direct connection between loneliness and stress. Cacioppo's work showed clear correlations between extremely high levels of cortisol and feelings of loneliness, demonstrating a definite link between loneliness and stress. He then compared the cortisol levels of lonely people with the cortisol levels of assault victims. He found the cortisol levels of the two groups to be the same. Cacioppo's work clearly shows that being lonely is as stressful as being the victim of a physical attack. Cacioppo then decided to find out if anyone else had studied the physical effects of loneliness. He found Professor Sheldon Cohen's research, which demonstrates that lonely people are three times more likely to catch a cold than people who are socially connected. And epidemiologist, Lisa Berkman's research, which showed that if you're lonely, you're two to three times more likely to die than people who aren't lonely. Having found these remarkable research results, Cacioppo was inspired to conduct more of his own research, to study the links between loneliness and depression. He found that the majority of people who became depressed had first started to experience loneliness. His research clearly demonstrated that loneliness is one of the key causes of both anxiety and depression.

Each of these different studies produced remarkable results. But when considered together, you can see that the final conclusions from Cacioppo's investigation into the effects of loneliness have significant mental and physical health implications: Loneliness is a major cause of stress, anxiety and depression. It makes you two to three times more likely to become ill and die.

Hari concludes his discussion of this issue with an explanation of Cacioppo's solution to the problem: Loneliness can't be cured by just putting us around other people. Just as in the tragic cases of the babies who died from lack of human contact and interaction, it's not enough to just be around people, because our vital need isn't just for people.

Our vital fundamental need is *connection* with people.

That's why active listening had such a powerful impact on my life - because it fulfilled that vital human need. Providing the core conditions in my relationships with my clients in this way had strengthened the bonds and connections between us. And that also explained why things had changed so much at work for me. By focusing first and foremost on developing the relationships between me and my students and making a genuine connection with them, I'd unconsciously been meeting an essential human need - in both me and my students.

But why is it so important? Why do we need it so badly? What does connection do for us that's so crucial? The answer lies in our evolutionary history.

As mammals evolved from reptiles, one of the most significant changes was the change in the process of reproduction. Reptiles lay eggs, which are very often left without any further care from their parents. But mammals not only develop their young inside them; mammals' young also need a lot of continued care from their parents. Mammals' brains are bigger than reptiles', giving them more intelligence. However, this means their brains need more time to develop, leaving mammalian babies needing more parental care. To ensure that their babies would get the continued care they needed, mammals' brains developed entirely new sections, with entirely new functions. These new sections of the brain are known as the limbic system. A key function of the limbic system is to enable mammals to interpret the inner emotional states of other members of their species - to know how they're feeling. So, with regards to babies, our limbic systems enable us to be in tune with them, so we can understand their needs and ensure they're met. Our limbic systems evolved to enable us to connect with each other emotionally - to empathise with each other. They enable us to feel what other people are feeling, so we can understand and fulfil each others' needs. They enable us to love and care for each other - that's their purpose.

We're the end-product of the evolutionary design process: we're designed - *made* to nourish, love and care for each other, because we all need connection, love, care and affection, in order to survive.

That's what René Spitz found in his investigation into the deaths of orphaned children: it was the lack of what would usually be mothers' care, love and comfort, which led to their deaths. And that's also what John

Cacioppo found in his investigation into the effects of loneliness: without the nourishing companionship, care and affection of family, friends and partners, we're at major risk of illness and death.

And so, to ensure that we give and get these things we all need, we're born with the ability to tune in and connect with each other through our limbic brains - through a process known as 'limbic resonance'.

In '*A General Theory of Love*', Doctors Lewis, Amini and Lannon explain this little known, but fundamental aspect of what it means to be human. They explain how our emotional states are 'contagious', due to limbic resonance. Limbic resonance refers to the fact *that* we pass on our emotions to others, just as they also pass on their emotions to us. We literally feel what others are feeling, because we're connected to each other through our limbic systems, which are designed to be open and receptive to this emotional transmission.

If you've ever been to a major sporting event, you'll know how different it feels watching it in the stadium, compared to watching a big sporting event at home on the TV. It's *so* much better at a stadium. The difference is immense, because the atmosphere is so emotionally charged with the raised emotions of all the spectators who are sharing and passing on their emotions to each other, so that *everyone* in the stadium is feeling that same sense of excitement. When we pay to go to some large exciting event, we might think that we're paying all that money to be uplifted by the musicians, artistes or athletes who will perform, but in fact, we're also paying for the audience - all the other people around us, who make it special. We're paying to be gathered in one place with lots of other like-minded, positive-feeling people, because *that's* what makes it special - all those other people - passing on and sharing all that excitement - all that *emotion*.

But although it might be easier to recognise this emotional transmission when amongst a crowd of people, it actually happens all the time; it's just that we don't tend to be aware of it. I knew nothing of it and didn't realise it was even possible, until I started counselling. In counselling, it becomes much more apparent, because counsellors are deliberately focusing on being empathetic - on feeling what their clients are feeling. And it was when I was counselling Robert, who'd been the victim of a violent assault, that the truth and the power of this emotional connection became really clear to me.

Robert had been suffering from daily flashbacks of the assault, in which he re-experienced the full power of the emotions that were present during the assault. He'd explained how he often now felt extreme anxiety and panic when having to be out in public, because of the attack. During one counselling session, he described the assault to me in all of its horrifying detail, stating how terrifyingly close to death he'd felt. At the end of that session, after he'd left, I was feeling strange: a little shaky and emotional. I initially thought this was just because I was tired and had been told something which was horrible to hear. However, straight after that session, I'd arranged to go into town to meet a friend for drinks. When I got off the train, there were the usual Friday night groups of people around, in loud and lively spirits. But these lively people, with whom I would've normally felt some kind of kinship, now suddenly felt scary and threatening. I found myself in a state of extreme anxiety, feeling a growing sense of panic and an urgent need to be away somewhere quiet and safe. It wasn't until later, when I was sat with my friend, feeling relaxed (and safe), that I realised what had happened. Robert had transmitted his anxiety, fear and panic to me. I had received and was feeling all the same emotions he felt when out in public. The people who were out and around me had not been in any way threatening - they were just the usual office-workers celebrating the end of the week's work. And I'd never before felt threatened in that situation, just as I've never felt that way since. But on that night, because of Robert's transmitted emotions, I was almost shaking with fear.

Human connection sounds awful, if it means that we're going to experience other people's unpleasant emotions. But, although it wasn't pleasant to be feeling the anxiety and fear that Robert had passed on to me, it served a really important purpose. It enabled me to truly empathise with him, to share and understand what he was feeling.

But it wasn't just empathy; the connection between us enabled all of the 'core conditions' of the counselling relationship: unconditional positive regard (acceptance), empathy and congruence (authenticity).

The connection between us allowed for the possibility of healing to begin:

- Because of empathy, I could genuinely say, 'I know how you feel'.

- I could show him that his feelings of fear and anxiety were understandable and acceptable - that *he* was acceptable - that they didn't make him pathetic or worthless.

- He was then able to accept those feelings and therefore accept *himself*.

All of this happened because of connection - our fundamental, vital human need. Connection brings understanding, empathy, compassion, emotional healing, and mental wellbeing. Connection is therefore the basis of all effective counselling. But, not only that:

Connection is the basis and foundation of all human life.

The Nobel Peace Prize winner, Archbishop Desmond Tutu explains this fact perfectly, through the South African philosophy of 'Ubuntu'. He explains why love, compassion and empathy are essential components of our humanity. Ubuntu states that we only get to be a person, because of other people. Everything that we are, or become, depends on other people: We need other people to bring us into the world; we learn to speak, think and walk through other people. We *learn* to be human through other people, and we're only able to live at all, because of other people (24). That's why we owe all humans our love, compassion and empathy; because without human connection, we're nothing.

In '*A General Theory of Love*', Lewis, Amini and Lannon give a detailed explanation of why this is so. They demonstrate how human connection is essential for good physical and mental health: because limbic system connection between people not only transmits emotions, it also regulates our essential physiological systems, ensuring our bodies' vital systems are fully functioning.

This limbic regulation is most important when we're babies, during which time we totally depend on the close proximity of our mothers, whose presence regulates a number of key physiological functions, including breathing, sleep, hormones and immune systems. In the presence of our mothers, our infant bodies essentially 'learn' to regulate themselves, so that later in life, they can be more independent. But if babies are deprived of limbic connection with their mothers, they never gain these skills, so they die, as happened in the tragic cases I described earlier. However, although babies eventually become able to regulate themselves more independently as they grow older, this dependence on limbic regulation never entirely disappears. As adults, our bodies still benefit from limbic system connection and regulation.

In '*A General Theory of Love*', Lewis, Amini and Lannon explain how this limbic connection in adults is clearly demonstrated by two well-known phenomena: Firstly, the fact that women who live together often find that when they begin to share a household, their periods begin to synchronise. They eventually all menstruate at the same time each month - due to the limbic-system connection between them and the regulation of physiological systems that comes with it. And secondly, an even clearer demonstration of the presence and importance of limbic regulation in adults is the fact that, in a long-term marriage, if one partner dies, it's very often the case that that the other partner will die soon afterwards, due to the lack of limbic connection and regulation their bodies are used to and dependent on. When we hear of this, we often say that 'they died of a broken heart', without realising that it's essentially true. Without our husbands or wives beside us, our hearts 'break', or malfunction - along with the rest of our bodies' essential functions, because of the lack of limbic regulation and human connection.

So that also explains the findings of John Cacioppo into the effects of loneliness on our physical health: that loneliness makes you two to three times more likely to die, because without human connection, we're not only missing out on the care and affection of family, friends and partners, we're also missing out on the essential limbic regulation they provide.

When we're disconnected, our bodies send us powerful signals, by going into protest or despair mode - becoming flooded with adrenalin and cortisol, just as John Cacioppo discovered. Our bodies give us clear signals about what we need. That's why it feels so good to be with our friends, families and partners, because our bodies are rewarding us for giving them what they need, by releasing the pleasure hormones: dopamine, serotonin and oxytocin – the 'love drug'. That's why hugs are so pleasurable. That safe, warm, affectionate connection gives us a lovely big shot of pleasure hormones - so we'll enjoy it and want to do it again.

Our bodies very clearly signal to us what they need by making disconnection painful and connection pleasurable. So we need to listen to them and actively seek out new connections, and cherish and maintain our existing connections. Yes, that does mean doing things that may make you feel a little uncomfortable, like phoning that friend who you've not phoned for ages - the one you've been feeling guilty about. The truth is, you've been having guilty thoughts and feelings because it's true - you really should contact that friend! But now you know that contacting them will be really beneficial to both of you, there's nothing to stop you, is there? So go on - reach out, make contact – connect. That's what you are meant to do - made and designed to do.

Treasure your connections - your relationships with your workmates, neighbours, family and friends, because they're not only precious, they're essential. That's what researchers at Harvard University found, in their eighty-year study on happiness - the biggest study ever done on the subject: The key to a long, healthy and happy life is to maintain our connections and have good social and family relationships (25).

That's why it's so important to create the right (core) conditions to keep our relationships and connections alive and flourishing, as it's because of those relationships that *we* are all kept alive and flourishing. By applying the core conditions of unconditional positive regard, empathy and congruence to all your relationships, you become a positive force in the world, improving (and saving!) the lives of everyone around you.

So please, remember to practice creating these conditions, until you are a connection 'black-belt' - a connection 'master'. Practice, as if the health and happiness of your loved ones depends upon it, as if *your* life depends upon it, because it does.

You can change your life

We are all a product of our experience

If you treat people like good people, they will *be* good people

We are all on a journey

Changing the way we behave, changes us

The relationship is the therapy

We are meant to be connected

Exercise:

Make three connections with old friends this week.

Chapter 7: Connect- for a Minute

We're meant and made to be connected, designed to love and care for each other. So our close connections are hugely important. But brief connections of just a couple of minutes, or saying hello to a neighbour, colleague, or passing stranger can also have a surprisingly significant impact on our lives. They can also play a key part in your journey of becoming who you want to be - who you're born and meant to be.

A great example of the power and potential of brief connections is the organisation and movement started by Igor Kreyman in 2016 called *'The Human Connection Movement'* (26). Kreyman was concerned by the disconnected nature of modern life, which he knew was causing somewhat of an epidemic of loneliness and its accompanying mental and physical health problems. Starting in Australia, but then going on to involve thousands of people across the world, Kreyman organised 'eye-gazing events' which brought together strangers in various public venues around the world to sit and look into each other's eyes for as long as they felt comfortable - often for no longer than one or two minutes. And across the world, regardless of who was paired with who, the results were the same: people reported feeling not only connected with the stranger opposite them, they also reported feelings of affection and love.

This effect was first noted back in 1989 in an experiment by the psychologists Joan Kellerman, James Lewis and James D. Laird (27). In this experiment, just as in the eye-gazing events, strangers were asked to look into each other's eyes for two minutes, after which, they reported feelings of passionate love for each other! Since then, advances in neuroscience have enabled us to see what's happening when we make eye contact in this way: we experience enhanced neural synchronization in brain areas relating to empathy and social connection. We also tend to synchronise blinking, pupil-dilation and breathing with those whom we have eye-contact with, once again, demonstrating some of the possibility and power of human connection. But don't just take my word for it - try this experiment yourself, with your spouse, partner or friend. It's a great way to reignite or deepen your connection and relationship.

Amnesty International, the world's leading human rights organisation, was so taken with the results of these experiments that they set up their own, in a project called '*Look beyond Borders*' (28). This project put together refugees from Syria and Somalia with Europeans, in order to demonstrate an essential truth which eye-gazing reveals: when you look beyond the superficial markers of identity which normally separate us, like gender, social class, religion, ethnicity, age or nationality, that underneath these differences, we're essentially all the same, experiencing the same emotions, the same vulnerabilities, and sharing the same need for human connection. And just as was seen in the eye-gazing events organised by the Human Connection Movement, it didn't matter which kind of person was paired with which other kind. In each and every case, connection happened. Connection happened between all these seemingly different people, because underneath it all, they're not different; they're all the same - all human.

So, when you look at, or think about the people around you, at work, or in your neighbourhood, don't think that you have nothing in common with them, and no way to connect with them. You have the very essence and basis of who you are in common with them - your humanity.

We may have lived and be living different lives. We may have different religions, languages, and different ideas about music, entertainment, food, relationships, politics, clothes, work and money. But these are all just products of our experience; just superficial differences brought about by growing up and living in different families, countries or communities from each other. Knowing that we're all products of our experience, we can put aside the judgements that might come to mind about different people's opinions and behaviour and seek to understand and empathise instead. We can remember that, even if their behaviour or their opinions seem different or 'bad', that doesn't mean that *they* are bad.

You have good people all around you - if you can just see them and treat them as such. You have good people all around, with whom you have so much in common - your common humanity. You have people around you who it would be good to connect with - good for you and good for them. So go on - reach out, make contact – connect - that's what you are meant, made and designed to do.

But, don't worry, I am not suggesting that you have to run out and 'force' people to eye-gaze with you! Connection doesn't always have to be that intense, in order for it to be meaningful or important. Connection can start with and may consist of nothing more than a simple and straightforward 'hello'; the branch of psychotherapy known as 'Transactional Analysis' understands this.

Transactional Analysis (TA) focuses on analysing interactions between individuals. TA understands and very effectively explains people's basic need for connection with, and attention from other people. In their book, *'TA Today'* (29), Ian Stewart and Vann Joines explain how in early childhood, the attention and connection that people need is physical. But as adults, our needs change: we don't just want and need physical attention and connection; we also crave recognition from other people - recognition of our existence. Within TA, this is known as 'recognition hunger'. The reason we hunger for recognition of our existence, is because recognition from other people is essentially, a recognition and acknowledgement of our worth. This theory of 'recognition hunger' echoes the view of Dale Carnegie, regarding the fundamental aspect of human nature which he explained in *'How to Win Friends and Influence People'*; that we all have a craving to feel good about ourselves - to feel that we have worth.

In *'TA Today'*, Stewart and Joines describe how we go about satisfying this hunger and need for recognition, by giving and receiving what, in TA, is called 'strokes'.

In TA, a 'stroke' is a 'unit of recognition'. For example, if we passed by a neighbour in the street and said 'hello' to them, we would be giving them a 'stroke' - a 'unit of recognition', because by saying hello, we've recognised their existence. When they return this greeting, we then receive a stroke from them, because they've recognised our existence. This little exchange of strokes gives us both a little boost, because we've recognised each other's existence and worth. And because it's a friendly exchange, it's said that we've exchanged 'positive strokes'. Additionally, if we'd stopped to talk and pass the time, we would've given each other more positive strokes, because we'd given each other more attention - more recognition of each other's worth. However, it's also possible to receive 'negative strokes' from less pleasant interactions, such as when we receive criticism or insults. Therefore, to maintain our overall sense of wellbeing, we need to receive more positive than negative strokes. This is because we all possess an internal 'stroke bank', a kind of unconscious internal tally of and feeling for the amount of positive and negative strokes we have received. Although we won't be consciously aware of the exact state of our stroke-bank, we'll still be affected by our stroke-bank balance. If we've received more positive than negative strokes, we'll feel a greater sense of wellbeing, feeling more happy and content.

But you already know this is true. You know that when you exchange smiles, eye-contact or hellos with people, you always feel just a little more chirpy and cheerful afterwards. I always notice this when going into work. I might initially feel a little tired, and maybe a little stressed or unhappy, but after having exchanged a few cheery 'good mornings' with my colleagues, I always feel a bit brighter and better for it. Similarly, one thing I love about going for a walk in the countryside or park is exchanging smiles and good mornings with passers-by, which always warms my heart and gives me a little lift and 'spring in my step'.

So we can see that even the smallest and briefest of connections can be important; just a five-second exchange of greetings can have a positive effect on the wellbeing of you and those you meet, because of the giving and receiving of positive strokes - that recognition of each other's existence and worth. In much of the western world, we're not always aware of this, possibly because of how we greet each other when we meet. We mainly tend to greet people by saying something like 'hi' or 'hello', so the significance of this exchange isn't really apparent. However, in other parts of the world, there are greetings which show much more understanding of the power and importance of these small, everyday connections.

If you travel to South Africa, you may hear the traditional Zulu greeting of 'sawubona', which means 'I see you, you are important to me and I value you' (30). The traditional Hindu greeting of 'namaste' does something similar; as it means 'I bow to the divine in you', recognising and acknowledging what is believed to be the divine spark or essence that is said to be present in all of us.

The meanings of these greetings - these alternative versions of 'hello', or 'hi', demonstrate the truth of TA's theory of positive strokes - that when we say hello to each other, we're recognising each other's existence and worth. Therefore, in essence, when we say hello, we're actually saying sawubona, or namaste; saying 'I see you', you are important to me and I value you', or 'I bow to the divine in you'.

This gives us another way to understand the damaging effects of loneliness and its role in causing depression. Without human connection - even those little five-second connections of a shared 'hello'; we lack that vital recognition and acknowledgement of our worth and existence. Without that, we may not only feel that we have no worth, we may also feel that as our existence is unrecognised, then our existence has no worth - that it would be better if we were dead. Lack of human connection is a major cause of loneliness. Loneliness is a major cause of depression and depression is a major cause of suicide; approximately 66% of people who committed suicide had first experienced depression.

So, never underestimate the power and the potential impact that your little hello could have on the lives of those around you. In just saying hello to your neighbour, your colleague, or that person you always pass on the street; in that one small connection - that one gift of a positive stroke and recognition of their existence and worth, you may actually be a life-saver.

So please, reach out; treat people like they are good people; recognise their existence and worth: smile, make eye-contact, say hello. Because before you know it, our hello can become 'how are you?', and 'how are you?' becomes a conversation - a connection, an enriching exchange of positive strokes, a recognition of each other's essential worth and a source of warm nourishment for our greater physical and mental wellbeing.

By reaching out in this way, you're continually practicing and applying the philosophy which makes you a better person – the person you want to be. You're now going way beyond the practice of just turning this philosophy on and off for conversations. You're now making this your standard operating procedure – your way of life. You're actively and consciously focused on being a continual positive presence and force in the world. You're making this who you are.

In a world in which the human population is soon predicted to reach eight billion, it's easy to feel insignificant and unimportant. In a world in which our media constantly celebrates the rich and famous, it's easy to feel that we don't matter. But the truth is, you *do* matter. **You can make a difference to every person you meet**. And you can start today. You can start right now.

You can change your life

We are all a product of our experience

If you treat people like good people, they will *be* good people

We are all on a journey

Changing the way we behave, changes us

The relationship is the therapy

We are meant to be connected

You can make a difference to every person you meet

Exercise:

Say hello/make conversation with ten strangers this week

Chapter 8: Connection - with Everyone.

We're all shaped by our relationships and connections. But that's not the only way we're a product of our experience – not the only thing that's made us who we are. We're also fundamentally affected by the kind of society we grow up and live in. This is the key focus and foundational insight of sociology: We're all shaped by the experience of growing up and living according to the ideas and values of our culture, what Carl Rogers would call the 'conditions of worth' imposed by our society.

Every society is a complex system. But although complex, at their heart, they're a system of relationships between their members. Viewing them this way enables us to see how Rogers' ideas, regarding how to make our relationships more healthy and therapeutic, can also be applied to the organisation of our societies. So although this societal focus means we're now plotting a different course than in the previous chapters, please bear with me. It's in the application of these ideas to the organisation of our communities and culture, that we may be able to see the greatest improvements in every aspect of our lives.

Understanding our society as a system of relationships means we can have some idea about how to create the right conditions for us all to thrive - for us all to connect and bring out the best in each other. At present, it's too often the case that our societies separate, rather than connect us. They put distance between us – dividing us with competition, conflict and mutual distrust over superficial differences such as class, ethnicity and nationality. This means we never have the opportunity to see and realise the true value and worth of all the people around us, because we're all so disconnected.

However, I think this is beginning to change. I think there are some sparkling glimmers of hope appearing. And strangely, these glimmers of hope first appeared during one of the most difficult times of our recent history - during the 'lockdown' - the official isolation policy put in place by the government, in order to contain the coronavirus pandemic.

During lockdown, those not working in essential services had to 'stay home and save lives'. We weren't allowed to go out to meet with friends, family or partners who didn't live with us. Most of us weren't allowed to go to work, so we couldn't see our work-mates. We weren't allowed to see all those people we had connections with. And we couldn't go out and make new connections either, because all pubs, bars, restaurants and leisure centres were locked down too. We were confined to our homes. And for those of us who lived alone, that meant solitary confinement. Solitary confinement is used as the worst punishment in prisons. It's torture, as it deprives us of that fundamental human need - connection.

We really missed that connection. And as the weeks of lockdown went on, that missing just grew and grew, till we began to really hunger for it. In every conversation I had with friends and family at that time, everyone talked about it. But that turned out to be a good thing, because we began to realise and really appreciate how much we love and need our friends and family. So we acted on that love, making that extra effort to reach out to those people we were missing. We were phoning, face-timing, Skype-ing, and Zoom-ing, connecting like we hadn't always done before, because now, suddenly, we really appreciated how important it was. But that wasn't all, in our hunger for connection; we were now reaching out to strangers as well. During the daily hour's exercise that we were allowed to have outside every day, people were suddenly much friendlier than they'd been before. Strangers were now much more likely to smile, say hello and even start up a conversation - sharing positive strokes, to meet that hunger and need. We were now suddenly realising how much we all needed other people.

And what was equally hopeful, was how everyone began to see and understand some of the fundamental connections they already shared with everyone in our society. It started to become clear that we're already inter-connected and inter-dependent in so many ways.

It started of course, with our National Health Service - the NHS. Suddenly, everyone was reminded of its value, of how important doctors and nurses were. There was a great demonstration of this in the little ex-mining village where I live. Driving down the main road became like a carnival trip, with flags and banners in every front garden, all celebrating the NHS' vital work. That was great to see. What came next was even better.

People began to see how *everyone* in the health service was important - not just doctors and nurses, but everyone, including, especially, those people doing jobs which previously were too often seen as low-status and unimportant. So now receptionists, hospital porters, cleaners, admin staff - everyone was now seen as a 'key worker' - a vital member of society. We now began to properly see the value of everyone, in every different job. Everyone was important - a 'key worker', because everyone in every different job was needed, in order for our health service to continue doing its vital work.

But it didn't end there. The understanding of people's importance shifted even more, as people realised it wasn't just NHS workers who we depended on. People started to realise that lots of other people in lots of other jobs were key workers too. So now we all began to realise the true value of care workers, refuse collectors, truck drivers, delivery drivers, warehouse operatives, farmers, fruit pickers, shelf stackers, supermarket workers, teachers, childminders - the list is almost endless and I haven't exhausted it here.

We began to realise what was really important in our lives and *who* was really important in our society. We began to realise that all of our lives were totally dependent on the work of these 'ordinary' people, doing their jobs, without whom, we couldn't survive. Every time I went to the supermarket, I noticed this change. People were now much more appreciative of the staff who worked there. And I saw delivery drivers who brought the weekly shopping to those who were self-isolating being treated like a new emergency service, and given the corresponding levels of respect, thanks and praise which went with that new status. We were waking up to an entirely new 'reality'.

We were beginning to realise that the people who we're normally made to believe are most important, actually, aren't that important at all. Suddenly, so many of the stars and celebrities who the media tell us to look up to, found themselves replaced by the real 'stars' of our society. It was the ordinary people who were important - people just going about their ordinary lives, doing their ordinary, but actually vitally-important jobs. These people were the real heroes of our society.

Politicians suddenly seemed less significant too. Parliament shut down, but hospitals, care homes and supermarkets didn't. All those places providing essential services stayed open because they were truly important, as were all the people who worked in them.

Some key truths were being revealed about who and what really mattered in our society. As documented by Yuval Noah Harari, in his global bestseller *'Sapiens: A Brief History of Humankind'* (31): Harari showed that most of the history of humankind which we're continually fed by mainstream sources is really just the history of that tiny percentage of people who've actually done nothing but preyed on, and leached off the work of the rest of humanity. Throughout our entire history, the really important people are always those who we depend on for the everyday necessities of life. Ordinary people, doing their ordinary jobs, growing food, tending cattle, building houses etc., providing the essentials of life; these are and always have been the real heroes of humanity.

But this truth which the pandemic revealed is actually just the tip of the iceberg. Realisation of our dependence on and connection to those 'key' workers in our society, points to and reveals an even deeper truth, about the real level of inter-connection and inter-dependence in society. This was first documented by another world-famous academic, Emile Durkheim, in 1893, in his seminal work '*The Division of Labour in Society*' (32). Durkheim demonstrated that we're actually all connected to and dependent on every other person in society.

Durkheim documented the major changes to our ways of living that came with the Industrial Revolution. This was when we moved from the simple and mainly self-sufficient life of the countryside, to the much more complex life of the industrial towns and cities. Durkheim noted that before the Industrial Revolution, we were all very self-sufficient, meaning that we all had to be a 'Jack of all trades'. Within our family units, we grew our own food, educated our children, tended our own livestock, built our own houses, and provided care for ill or infirm family members. But when the Industrial Revolution came, we stopped working for ourselves and instead, we went to work for others. We earned a wage to buy the things we needed, rather than providing those things for ourselves. So now, instead of being a 'Jack of all trades' and doing everything ourselves, we now just did the one job that we were employed and paid for. But we could only live that way, because we knew that everyone else was doing every other job that needed to be done. We now worked as a team, with everyone else in society, all relying and dependent on each other.

Since Durkheim's time, industry, business and society have become ever-more complex. Life's become more complex and jobs have become ever-more specialised. This means Durkheim's observations are even more relevant now than they were when he was alive; because of that specialisation.

There are so many more different kinds of jobs around now than there were in Durkheim's time. In every area of life, every job has become much more specialised. So, for example, you're now much less likely to employ a general builder – you'd employ all the different building specialists, such as bricklayers, carpenters and plumbers etc. If you're ill, although you may initially go to the local doctor - the 'general practitioner'; you may then be sent to see a specialist, such as a physiotherapist, chiropractor, or optician. As we specialise into ever-more narrow areas of work, we therefore become ever-more dependent on everyone else doing their jobs, in order for us to not only survive - but also thrive. Because increasing specialisation means there's an ever-increasing variety of different jobs and careers available. This then makes it much more possible and likely that we can find a job which really suits our particular individual tastes, attitudes, values, temperament, character, skills and qualities. And because the job suits us so well, it's much more likely that we'll be more content, fulfilled and well-paid.

We're led to believe that people in a well-paid and fulfilling job are only successful because of their individual hard work and ability. Therefore, they owe no debt of gratitude to anyone but themselves. But Durkheim's work clearly shows that this is entirely false. Those people who are successful in their specialist line of work owe everything to everyone else in society. Without everyone else doing their jobs, it wouldn't have been possible for any area of speciality to exist in the first place, or for anyone to then become 'expert' and gain all the rewards that come with that specialist skill and expertise. And so if we're in a successful job, we not only owe the existence of our job to everyone else in society; we also owe our satisfaction and wealth to them as well.

None of us have the knowledge and ability to be self-sufficient anymore, because life's become so specialised and complex. We all need each other. Our lives and our society are made up of an ever-more complex web of connections between all the different specialised jobs that have to be done, in order for us all to thrive. And taken as a whole, on average, our modern, technologically advanced societies really are thriving. We're all, on average, much wealthier and healthier than before, because of that ever-increasing specialisation.

When we lived much more self-sufficient lives, before the Industrial Revolution, we had to be a 'Jack of all trades'. As we had to be able to do every job, we never got the chance to become really good at any one particular job - to become 'master of one'. But now, we get to specialise, focus and concentrate on being as good as we can at just one job. That means that in every area of work, we keep improving, keep advancing and keep developing new skills, knowledge, expertise, technology and new and more efficient ways of doing things. In all areas of life, there's constant development and advancement - because of specialisation. It's specialisation that's made our societies so advanced and brought all the improvements in health and wealth which we all benefit from. But specialisation means inter-dependence. One cannot exist without the other.

And although it's true that certain individuals' inventions and entrepreneurial innovations have brought great benefits to us all, those individuals could never have achieved what they did in their own specialist fields without being able to depend on every other person in society doing their jobs. We're all intricately and inextricably connected to and dependent on every other person in our society for our ever-increasing levels of health, wealth and (hopefully) happiness. We therefore all owe all of this health, wealth and happiness to everyone else in our society.

That's pretty mind-boggling, isn't it?

But we're not just connected to everyone in our society; we're also connected to everyone around the world. Just take a look at anything around you that's been manufactured. Look at where it was made. The chances are very high that it was made somewhere like China or India - not in your country. So we've now become dependent on people all around the world to get the things we want and need. This means that we also owe them a debt of gratitude, because once again, by them specialising and doing those jobs, it means that we're able to specialise and do our jobs. In modern technologically-advanced societies, there are an ever-growing number of high-paid, high-skill jobs, with a corresponding decrease in low-skill, low-waged manufacturing jobs. But this societal specialisation which has brought so much wealth to advanced societies is only possible, because the lower-paid and lower-skilled manufacturing work is being done elsewhere. In the same way that we're dependent on people in our own society, we're now also dependent on people in every other society. We're now connected to and dependent on everyone, everywhere.

We're utterly dependent on our connections. We depend on our friends, families, partners, neighbours and workmates for our health and happiness. We're dependent on every member of our society, through the societal division of labour, for our health, wealth, happiness and our very existence. Through the global division of labour, our lives are now connected to and dependent on, every other person around the world.

Connection is the basis and foundation of all human life.

So we need to recognise and acknowledge that connection and the debt we owe to everyone we depend on. We need to honour and reward the real heroes of our societies: the ordinary people, doing their ordinary, but vital jobs. To honour that debt, we have a duty to ensure that we create the right conditions for everyone to self-actualise and become the very best that they can be. We have to do this for one another, because **we all need one another**. We're enmeshed in complex webs of interconnection and interdependence with everyone. What you do matters. *You* matter, because people are dependent on you. *Everyone* matters, because we're all dependent on everyone else. Therefore, if we want to make meaningful and lasting improvements to our lives, we know we have to help and enable others to do the same to theirs. We have to stop thinking of 'them' and 'us', because there is no 'them', just us. We are all connected, all one.

So now it's time to start behaving that way…

You can change your life

We are all a product of our experience

If you treat people like good people, they will *be* good people

We are all on a journey

Changing the way we behave, changes us

The relationship is the therapy

We are meant to be connected

You can make a difference to every person you meet

We all need one another

Exercise:

Next time you make a drink such as tea or coffee, try to trace back all the people who were involved in it – from the tea or coffee, milk, sugar, crockery, kettle, spoon etc.

Chapter 9: A Society Fit for Heroes

Ask yourself, and be as honest as you can: have you really fulfilled your potential? Have you self- actualised? For many of us, I'd guess the answer would be 'not entirely', or 'not at all'. Why is that? Maybe we either consciously or unconsciously limited what we aimed, dreamed and strived for. Maybe we were never instilled with a belief in our potential: in our upbringing, education, community or society.

Who could you be, and what could you do if you had the chance? What could you dream of being?

Would you like to live in a society that made you believe that dream was achievable and was set up so that it really is? Would you like to 'live the dream' and have everyone else do the same? It might sound implausible, or impossible, but it's not.

Admittedly though, we're currently quite a long way away from realising that vision. At present, our societies are not designed for optimum human flourishing.

We live in grossly unequal and unfair societies, in an incredibly unequal and unfair world. In 2016, Oxfam reported that the richest 1% of the world's population now have more wealth than the rest of the world combined. The richest 26 people in the world have more wealth than the poorest 4000,000,000 people in the world (33). In May 2020, Forbes, the American business magazine, reported that the 25 richest people in the world became 255 billion dollars richer during the first two months of the global coronavirus pandemic (34).

Oxfam report that this inequality is not in any way inevitable; it's a direct result of government policies, which have deliberately favoured the wealthy, whilst disadvantaging everyone else, particularly the poorest in society. This is a global trend, which has seen the wealthiest siphon off most of the world's wealth, whilst the rest of the world's population suffers not only inequality, but also increasing insecurity.

Why does this matter? As long as everyone has enough to eat, then why does it matter that some people are much richer than others?

Professor Richard Wilkinson, in his book, '*The Impact of Inequality*', explains how and why inequality is so damaging. Wilkinson's book is based on thirty years of statistical analysis of global trends in inequality. His in-depth analyses reveal a startling and shocking truth: inequality in wealth always leads to inequality in health (35).

The most profound example of this trend is to be found in the United States, which is the richest country in the world and spends more on healthcare than any other country. But in the global rankings of life expectancy, the United States is currently at number forty-six. The situation in the UK is quite similar. The UK is number six in GDP, but twenty-nine in life expectancy. In comparison, Greece is ranked at number fifty-five in GDP, but number nineteen in life expectancy. Greece is significantly poorer, but significantly more equal in the distribution of wealth amongst its citizens. Wilkinson therefore demonstrates that it is not the overall level of wealth in a country which is important for its citizens' health and happiness - it is inequality in wealth which is the deciding factor.

These are not the only problems caused by inequalities in wealth. Wilkinson demonstrates how countries with high levels of wealth inequality also suffer from much higher rates of infant mortality, physical and mental illness, stress, anxiety and depression, and higher levels of crime, homicide, addiction, drug misuse, and higher percentages of the population in prison.

Unequal societies are quite simply sick societies, damaging to the well-being of their citizens. And although everybody loses out when their society is unequal, it's the poorer sections of society which lose the most. Many of the people who we rely on for our very existence have their lives shortened by the effects of inequality. For example, in the UK, average life expectancy in the poorest boroughs of London is around seventeen years less than for those who live in the wealthiest boroughs. Residents of the poorer areas will also experience much higher levels of physical and mental ill-health than the residents of the richer areas.

But inequalities in wealth also represent inequalities in social status. Low-paid jobs are also lower-status jobs. People in well-paid jobs are seen as better people, more valuable and worthy of respect than everyone else. But in unequal societies like ours, whilst the rich are constantly admired and praised, poorer people are constantly made to feel they're inferior.

As I write this, it brings up a long-buried memory, which even now makes me feel uncomfortable: I remember one of the first jobs I had after I left school, as a road-worker, laying gas and water pipes. I hated it. I felt like I was the lowest of the low – fit for nothing but the most menial labour. I remember feeling such a burning sense of shame when doing this job that I hid my face whenever I thought that someone I knew might see me. I should have been proud. I was helping to provide vital services. But instead, I was consumed by shame and humiliation, tormented by the lowly status which my society had allocated to my occupation.

This kind of status inequality leads to much higher levels of mental and physical illness. When you feel inferior, you're much more likely to experience stress, anxiety and depression. This has a hugely detrimental effect on the body's immune system. When we're stressed, our bodies' survival systems are in a constant state of high alert - in the fight, flight or freeze response. This diverts vital energy away from the body's immune systems, leading to much higher levels of both sickness and mortality amongst the working classes.

So we're hurting those who we should be helping. And hurting them means we're hurting ourselves. The coronavirus lockdown showed us that we're all important. But, in unequal societies, those on lower wages are made to feel inferior and worthless. And that's what causes so many social problems.

But, the most damaging effect of inequality, may be the suffering experienced by the whole planet, because of unequal societies.

Professor Wilkinson states that the most materialistic societies - those with the highest levels of consumer spending, are also the most unequal societies. Unequal societies make us all feel insecure about our status and worth. Because of this, we spend a huge amount of money on consumer goods, in order to demonstrate and prove to ourselves and everybody else that we have some value and worth. Advertisers know this and deliberately target our insecurities, so as to get us to buy consumer goods. Adverts are designed to make us feel insufficient: insufficiently attractive, cool, fashionable, sexy, successful, rich, powerful, healthy, and happy. They do this in order to then persuade us that we *will* be attractive, cool, fashionable, sexy, successful, powerful, healthy and happy - *if* we just buy their products. And it's this rampant consumerism, driven by inequality and insecurity, which is ravaging the planet. We devour ever-more natural resources, in a never-ending quest for the material sources and badges of self-satisfaction and self-worth; the self-satisfaction and self-worth which our unequal societies deny us.

Unequal societies are damaging to everyone, regardless of whether they're rich or poor, or whether their society is equal or unequal. It's therefore imperative that we create fairer and more equal societies in which everyone is valued and made to feel worthwhile. The fate of the entire world depends upon this.

But as it's political decisions which increase inequality, it's entirely possible for the right political decisions to be made which can equalise and improve our lives.

A good place to start making these changes is in education, to create societies designed for self-actualisation. We need to put education, training, and opportunities for lifelong self-development at the heart of our societies. The late Ken Robinson, an expert on global education reform, led the campaign to radically reform our education systems. He stated that our education systems are no longer fit for purpose - if they ever were (36). Robinson noted that an estimated one hundred billion people have lived on our planet, all of them individuals, possessing their own individual personalities, characters, temperaments, aptitudes, abilities and qualities. Diversity is one of the key characteristics of the human race. Unfortunately, our education systems, which we rely upon to develop people's abilities and realise their potential, don't recognise this. They only recognise, acknowledge, develop and reward a very narrow range of human abilities. They focus almost entirely on traditional academic subjects and skills. They also only enable expression of that narrow range of knowledge and skills in an incredibly limited fashion - mainly through written tests and essays. This completely disregards and negates the huge and diverse range of alternative skills, talents, aptitudes and abilities which don't fit this ridiculously restrictive view of human possibility. There is a famous quote, which is generally attributed to Albert Einstein, which sums this up perfectly: *"Everybody is a genius. But if you judge a fish by its ability to climb a tree, it will live its whole life believing that it is stupid."*

Sir Ken Robinson believed that if we can just create the right conditions, then every single person can find and develop their genius – their particular individual strengths and abilities. But these strengths are often not immediately apparent - we have to find them. And the only way to find them is to create the right conditions for them to be found.

That's what we need, but it's not what we've got. Most developed societies in the world have education systems which favour and benefit the wealthier middle and upper classes, whilst disadvantaging the rest. For example, in the UK, nearly all of the top positions in society are occupied by the wealthiest 7% of the population who went to private, fee-paying schools. Many of these private schools are traditionally named as 'public' schools. This is not because they're open to the general public. Public schools gained that name because they are designed to train the future elites for public service – for roles at the head of government. Public-school graduates dominate the higher status positions in society because they've been inculcated with the belief that they are the elite and are born to, and most capable of, ruling and running our society. Contrast this with the life and experience of a child born to unemployed parents, living in deprivation, in subsidised social housing and attending an overcrowded and underfunded school. How can a child from this background have any hope or aspiration of realising their potential? To aim for something better, we have to believe that we have some hope of achieving it. This is unlikely, if you grow up in poverty, in a house with no books, no working adults, in a neighbourhood where few people are working - never mind being successful.

That lack of belief was one of my biggest problems. Just getting to the point where I could even imagine I might possibly go to university at all was a massive hurdle. Whenever I was in town, and I walked past the grand, imposing university buildings, I used to feel as if there was some kind of invisible force-field around them, designed to repel and push people like me away. I felt like it was another world, an exclusive club to which I could never gain entry. Thanks to the brilliant lecturers on the Access course I attended, I eventually overcame that feeling and gained a place at university. But I still suffered from 'imposter syndrome'. I always felt that I didn't really belong – that at any moment someone would tap me on the shoulder and say, 'come on, out you go, this place isn't for the likes of you'.

We have to believe we have some worth and value, in order to have any hope or belief that we might be able to do anything worthwhile. Currently, our societies are not set up to help everyone believe in, discover, recognise and realise their potential. Intelligence is evenly spread across all social groups, but opportunity isn't. That's a tragic waste of talent. Although our modern levels of wealth-creation and technological sophistication are unparalleled in history, we have only just scratched the surface of our true human potential. Our greatest resource lays dormant, unexplored, undiscovered and under-developed.

However, if we can create education systems and societies that recognise the value and worth in everyone, we can create the right conditions for universal human thriving and self-actualisation. That's what we need, for the wellbeing and full development of every single individual in every single country, for human flourishing and fulfilment across the whole world.

We all want a better world, but what does that mean? When we say that, we don't really mean a better natural world, because the natural world is already wondrous and beautiful - except when humans ruin it. No, when we say we want a better world, we mean a better human world. Making a better human world means making humans better. And we know how to make humans better - we just have to create the right conditions.

In his hugely important and influential 'Stanford Prison Experiment', Phillip Zimbardo (37) demonstrated how everyone is capable of evil, if the conditions of their life push them towards that. In his experiment, Zimbardo found that placing people who'd previously thought themselves to be 'good', in the role of prison guard, quickly led to abuse of that power and sadistic treatment of those in the role of prisoner. But, crucially, Carl Rogers' research demonstrated the flip-side of this, showing that everyone is a good person – even the convicted prisoners he worked with, if given the chance to be. People are what we make them – they're a product of their experience and environment. If we create the right conditions, then we can get the best version of humanity, in the best kind of societies, where everyone can thrive, flourish, be happier, healthier and wealthier.

Making our societies more equal in levels of wealth, income and opportunity would benefit us in so many ways. We would see huge reductions in crime, violence, addiction, homelessness, mental and physical ill-health, and unemployment. The huge economic savings to every society which came from the reduction of these problems would also be majorly beneficial. We'd be doing much less damage to the planet, as we'd have much less desire and need to endlessly consume material goods, in a never-ending quest to feel worthwhile. Those are massive benefits, but there is even more that can be gained. If we create the right conditions for every single person to realise their potential, we could make something truly miraculous.

Imagine a society where every single person had the chance to find out what they were really good at and what they liked the most: where everyone was able to discover their particular strengths, skills and qualities, then got the chance to find the job which reflected, required and developed those strengths, skills and qualities.

Imagine a world in which *all* human societies were designed to realise human potential and maximise self-actualisation. Imagine the amazing talent that would be unleashed - all the inventions, amazing technologies, feats of engineering and architecture, of craftwork, art, music, design, film and literature. Think of the everyday excellence we would see in every person in every job - in builders, teachers, nurses, doctors, drivers, retail workers, painters, decorators etc: every job done well, providing every service; every human need, as well as it could possibly be provided. In that world, every job would be done by someone who'd realised they liked that job and was really good at it. Every job and every service which every organisation provided would be done really well. And not only that, because every job was done by someone who liked their job and was good at it, that would mean in every job, in every area, there would be continual improvements - because we had the best people for every job, doing every job happily and well.

Imagine that: everyone happy, valued and fulfilled. Everyone doing a job they liked and were good at, so that everyone was always developing and improving their skills, therefore improving the service they provided, thereby improving their little part of the world: Everyone improving their little part of the world, meaning that every little part of the world would therefore be improved.

A better world is possible, if we can just create the right conditions.

You can change your life

We are all a product of our experience

If you treat people like good people, they will *be* good people

We are all on a journey

Changing the way we behave, changes us

The relationship is the therapy

We are meant to be connected

You can make a difference to every person you meet

We all need one another

A better world is possible

Exercise: Consider the political parties that operate in your society:

- Which parties are focused on creating a fairer and more equal society, with equal opportunities for everyone to self-actualise and succeed?
- Which parties' policies always create greater inequality, social division and suffering?

Chapter 10: The Answer to Life

There *is* an answer to life.

It's true; there is an answer - a way of thinking and being which makes sense of your life, gives it meaning and purpose, and creates a much better environment for everyone.

And when I say it's true, I mean it's 'The Truth' that's shared by all the major schools of thought which seek the answers to the human condition: in psychology, sociology, philosophy, throughout literature, legend and mythology, and in all the major religions and spiritual beliefs across the world and throughout our history.

It's an age-old and eternal truth. But unfortunately, as David Mitchell so powerfully illustrates in his book, *Cloud Atlas* (38), it seems that every generation has had to re- discover the same truths for themselves and fight the same battles over and over again. Mitchell's epic tale of reincarnation shows how human history has been an eternal cycle and recurrence of the battle of good versus evil in the soul of all human beings.

Our modern world is vastly different from all previous human societies, as our technological capabilities seem to grow exponentially, bringing greater and faster change than has ever been seen before. But in our pride and amazement at our unparalleled levels of technological sophistication, we can all too easily imagine ourselves advanced, improved and different from humans of the past, so it's easy to forget, ignore or discard the vital lessons that our culture and history have to offer. Ignorance of these lessons dooms us to learn them the hard way, dooms us to forever re-tread the tragic path which David Mitchell describes.

But, as Robert M. Pirsig demonstrated in his globally-bestselling classic: '*Zen and the Art of Motorcycle Maintenance*' (39), much of our modern western culture is built on the values and philosophy of ancient Greece. A study of their systems of thought not only reveals the debt we owe to them, in terms of the benefits of rational, scientific modes of thinking, it also makes evident the values which are the foundation of our morality, providing guidance and solutions for the eternal problems of human being.

A key value of ancient Greece was 'arête', meaning excellence and virtue. The goal of life was to pursue excellence and virtue in all that one did – to always aim at the highest good, to be the best that one could be. Pursuing the highest good was seen as striving for the best from oneself and the best for others – for one's family, community and society. Desiring and aiming for the best in this way came from the primary moral virtue – 'agape'. Agape is an ancient Greco-Christian term, which refers to the highest form of love. Agape is the unconditional love for all human beings, which seeks for the best in everyone and the best for everyone, regardless of background, status or circumstance. Living a life in pursuit of excellence and virtue, driven by a universal love for human beings, would lead to a state of 'eudemonia' – meaning the state of optimum human flourishing.

We can see how these ancient values have been rediscovered and regenerated through time to remain ever-relevant to our lives by examining the ideas of the most prominent and influential thinkers of more recent times. Friedrich Nietzsche's 'will to power' was the drive to achieve our higher selves and be all that we can be. The will to power is the drive for arête. Achieving arête means realising our potential: achieving self-actualisation and optimum human flourishing. And as Carl Rogers noted: self-actualisation is enabled by providing the core conditions in our relationships.

The highest goal and primary drive of all human life is enabled and fuelled by what Rogers termed the 'core conditions' of unconditional positive regard and empathy. However, later in his career, in his book *A Way of Being*,(40) Rogers revealed that what he actually meant by this was unconditional love, or agape.

Carl Rogers discovered this truth in his research and work as a psychologist, stating that everyone was struggling with the same problem - the problem of becoming themselves. He stated that the universal solution to this universal problem was a special kind of relationship, one in which the 'core conditions' were present. Rogers found that when he accepted, valued, and, essentially, *loved* people exactly as they were, they became better people. That was the key ingredient in all successful counselling. The answer to all of the problems that brought people to therapy and counselling was love. Rogers found that when he valued and prized his clients unconditionally, then his clients began to value themselves, especially the parts of them which had been damaged or repressed because of their childhood. They then began to move towards a more positive place in themselves, to become better people - who they were always meant to be. They became better because they began to realise their true worth and value. They could then realise what kind of life they should live, living according to their own values - not their parents'. When we start to live this way, that's when we begin to become the person we were born to be, our true and best selves.

Rogers' approach to therapy was so effective and influential, that it's now become the standard approach for all therapists. All counsellors and psychotherapists understand that it's the core condition of agape, which creates the right conditions for healing, growth and positive change to occur. It's unconditional love which enables everyone to become the best that they can be.

Rogers' ideas were based on an ancient and eternal truth – something which is present in, and is a crucial aspect of all major religions. Rogers' philosophy is based on 'The Golden Rule' that applies to all human life, a rule which features in the philosophical writings of Aristotle and Plato; a rule which is present in all of our sacred codes and guides to life.

The Golden Rule is to follow the command in the Bible to 'Love thy neighbour, as thyself'. It is to 'do unto others, as you would have them do unto you'. It means we must treat everyone with dignity and respect, to value and prize everyone equally.

The command in the Torah, tells us to 'love the stranger'. In the Islamic faith, there is the rule that 'No one is a believer until he loves for his brother what he loves for himself'. In Sikhism: I am a stranger to no one, and no one is a stranger to me. Indeed, I am a friend to all. In Confucianism: One word which sums up the basis of all good conduct... loving-kindness.

In 1993, the 'Parliament of the World's Religions', which included 143 leaders of all the World's leading faiths, declared an agreement on this universal Golden Rule, which was applicable to and agreed upon by all faiths (41).

All faiths, all religions, all sacred and holy guides to living all agree. This collected wisdom from thousands of years of human existence tells us that the best we can be and do is to follow the Golden Rule – to 'love thy neighbour as thyself.'

The Golden Rule is also the basis of our ethical codes of human rights. Our ideas of human rights are all based on the idea that every human being is of equal value and worth, all equally deserving of dignity and respect. The basis of our human rights is a universal brotherly/sisterly love, which values all people equally, regardless of their circumstances or background.

Whether you believe in God, in the philosophy of human rights, or in the results of research, the same truth and rule applies.

Guided by this Golden Rule, we can make a difference to everyone we meet, as it reminds us that we're all good people - if we're just given the chance to be. So we can make a difference to our neighbours with a hello - a 'sawubona', or a 'namaste', giving them that little 'positive stroke' and recognition of their worth. We can do the same with passing strangers, with people who serve us food in a restaurant, who staff the tills and the aisles in supermarkets, who listen to our complaints in customer service departments. We can make a difference to the lives of everyone we meet, interact, or have any kind of brief connection with. And that difference is love.

We can even make a positive difference to the lives of people we never meet, by remembering to always think and act with love. We can remember the lessons that the 'lockdown' taught us - that we're all inter-connected, inter-dependent, and all important. Everyone is our 'neighbour', so we have to love them like we love ourselves. This brings an understanding of the changes we have to make, to create a better society. Following the Golden Rule means creating a society that's designed to get the best out of all human beings - a society which values everyone and enables everyone to self-actualise and become the best that they can be.

Basing our relationships, our lives and the organisation of our societies on this principle will reduce the amount of physical and mental illness, crime, violence and homicide in our societies. It will reduce the amount of addiction, suicides, discrimination and prejudice, and injustice in the world. It will reduce the amount of money we have to spend on dealing with these problems. It will also reduce the harm that we do to the planet, through our out-of-control consumerism.

Basing every aspect of life on the Golden Rule could finally unleash and enable us to harness the true power and potential of the human race. Creating the right conditions for everyone to realise their value and worth, could enable everyone to self-actualise and realise their full potential. It could unleash an incredible surge of human creativity, imagination, innovation and invention, which could transform human life beyond all recognition. If we created societies in which every single person was valued and every single human strength, quality and ability was given the chance to be found, developed and fully realised, we could improve all of our lives, in all of our societies, across the whole world.

With love, we can change the world. That's what our history shows us. Some of the greatest changes, the greatest gains, the greatest victories achieved by our greatest and most inspirational heroes were done with love.

Mahatma Gandhi changed the world, by helping to bring an end to Britain's colonial enslavement and exploitation of India. Gandhi acted on the principle of *'Whenever you are confronted with an opponent, conquer him with love.'* He believed that we should *'hate the sin, but love the sinner'.* Gandhi believed that if you act with love, then you'll bring out the best in people, eventually making them see that they have to behave morally. Gandhi believed that love was the universal law of life, the highest law of humankind (42).

Nelson Mandela brought peace and reconciliation to his country through love. Mandela had every reason to hate those who'd imprisoned him for twenty-eight years, and enslaved, oppressed and killed so many of his people. He had every reason to hate and he had it in his power, once he became president of South Africa, to act on that hate and take revenge against the white minority who had done so much damage to his life, people and country. But he didn't do it. He knew that despite all the evils that the apartheid regime was responsible for, they were still people, and therefore, essentially good at heart. Mandela stated:

"No one is born hating another person because of the colour of his skin, or his background, or his religion. People must learn to hate, and if they can learn to hate, they can be taught to love, for love comes more naturally to the human heart than its opposite." (43).

Mandela could have brought civil war to his country, but instead, he brought peace and reconciliation. Mandela was driven by the same philosophy which inspired the speeches of Martin Luther King:

"Darkness cannot drive out darkness, only light can do that. Hate cannot drive out hate, only love can do that"... "Love is the only force capable of transforming

an enemy into a friend." (44). That's how Mandela united his fractured nation, transformed enemies into friends, and saved his country from civil war.

Martin Luther King inspired the whole world with that philosophy, for which he won the Nobel Peace Prize. He advanced the cause of racial equality, without ever resorting to violence or hate. So we can take inspiration from these most inspirational leaders who changed the world, with love.

We all want a better world. And by that, we mean a world in which humans are better. To make humans better we have to create the right conditions for that to occur. We have to *"Be the change we want to see in the world"*- just as Gandhi said.

We can be that change, because that's what we're designed to do. We're the end-point of the evolutionary design process which gave us the limbic system. Our limbic systems are designed to enable us to connect with each other, so that we can empathise with each other and feel what each other is feeling. We're made to connect, so that we can understand and then meet each other's needs: give each other the love, care and affection which we all need, if we're to survive and thrive.

So be a loving person, because that's what you're meant and made to do. By doing what you're meant and made to do, you get to become who you're meant and made to be. We're all on this Hero's Journey - striving to become the person we were born to be.

So here's how you get to be the Hero of your own life and the lives of everyone around you. Here's how you harness and unleash 'The Force' that's inside all of us - the self-actualising tendency. You can do this for everyone in your life, and crucially, for *yourself*, with love. Because the command to 'love thy neighbour as thyself' means we *have to* give the same love and acceptance to ourselves, as we strive to give to other people. This is the most important part of our Hero's Journey: the quest to face our greatest fears, battle and defeat our personal demons. Because only by facing up to and accepting who we really are, can we become who we're really meant to be.

Our greatest fear is that we *really are* worthless and no good. This is the fear that drives all our defensive behaviours; it's the awful possibility we can't bear to face. It's what triggers our angry response to criticism and the rage that comes from feeling disrespected or humiliated. We lash out and rage against these slights because we can't bear to admit to what they seem to imply – that we might be, or are, not good enough.

So how do we overcome this? How can we accept and love ourselves, when we, more than anyone else, are all-too-aware of our flaws?

The solution is simple, but not easy. You have to face the truth and acknowledge all your faults. This is hard. It's scary. But in the end, there's no choice, because the alternative is much worse. Believe me, I know, because for most of my life, I lived in that much worse place.

Life's been a constant struggle against the underlying core-belief that I was worthless and bad. I raged against this belief, in fear it was probably true. It destroyed all my relationships, as I lashed out in bitter and resentful anger at the slightest hint that I might've been disrespected. I was angry and bitter, because at heart, the disrespect felt deserved.

I seemed destined for a life without love. I definitely didn't love myself. I despised both myself, and the behaviours which then came from that. That's what turned self-hate into self-punishment. If I became aware that I was verbally lashing out at my partner, I'd then lash out at myself, violently. I'd punch myself repeatedly in the face, shouting, 'I hate me! Hate me! Hate me!' The inevitable end-result of this level of self-hatred was thoughts of suicide.

So, seeking understanding, desperate for change, I took a personality test. The test confirmed all of my worst fears – the truth of all my faults and flaws. Everything I hated about myself was confirmed as a key part of my personality. It was all there in black and white, revealing the ugly truth: I'm damaged; difficult to work with, live with, and love.

So maybe I was right to feel suicidal, because how could life be worthwhile, liveable, or even justified, if that's who I was?

Dejected and despairing, I looked back at my life, evaluating its worth, and mine. In that depressive emotional state, we tend to only see that which confirms it. I looked back, expecting confirmation and endless proof of my fatal flaws and unfitness for life.

But I couldn't find it.

Although I saw failed relationships and behaviour I was ashamed of, I also saw all the effort I'd put into trying to make some positive difference and be the best person I could be. And I saw the effects of that. I saw the students and counselling clients who I'd done my best to help. I remembered smiles and thanks which had come my way. And I couldn't deny any of it.

I couldn't deny the truth of the personality test, but I also couldn't deny the truth of the life I'd chosen and the person I'd strived to be. I didn't choose my genetic inheritance, upbringing and environment – didn't get to choose the 'cards' I'd been dealt by life. But I did choose what I'd do with those cards. And I couldn't help but be proud of that choice. So now, I can face the truth. I can admit to being flawed and difficult. But I can be proud of myself for being brave enough to face that. And I can be proud of what I've achieved despite my flaws. So now I can finally accept myself, truly and fully *be* myself and know that I'm worthwhile, in *all* that I am. I can stop being defensive, because there's no longer anything to defend against. I can start to give myself the acceptance and love that I've done my best to give to others.

And *you* can do the same. You can stop being defensive. You can stop acting out against criticism or signs of disrespect. You can stop defending and fighting against the secret fear that you're not good enough. You can face your demons, accepting the worst of yourself, because you know that despite those flaws, you're worthwhile – because you've chosen to be. You can fully accept yourself, self-actualise and really *be* yourself.

Because regardless of what you may've been before, you're now, by any-one's definition - a good and worthwhile person whose presence benefits the world. Remember Batman's message: It's not who you are that de-fines you – not your genetic inheritance or personality, *it's what you do*. By adopting love as your way of being, you have, through conscious choice and deliberate action, become a true force for good in the world. And this is a choice that's open to us all. We can accept and love ourselves, despite our flaws, because of the acceptance and love we strive to give to others. We can, and do, choose to love.

We can all make this choice, starting right now. We don't have to wish or wait for change - to wish that our politicians might do something to make a difference, because we can make and be that difference. We can all change and all make a change, starting right now, with every person we meet. We can love, appreciate, praise and thank our loved ones: our partners, children, family and friends for all that they are and do for us. We can pass out the 'positive strokes' wherever we go: to the reception-ist, the driver, the barista who makes our coffee, and with all our col-leagues, managers and workmates. We can spread the love - spread the 'feeling good' feeling everywhere. We can smooth and ease every inter-action, adding a little lubrication of appreciation into every encounter with another person. We can add a little love to every person's day: with every bit of care and affection: every smile, every 'good morning', every conversation, every bit of active listening - every little loving exchange with every person we meet. We can drop our little pebbles of love into the lives of all the people we know and meet and let that love ripple out through every person's every connection with every person they meet. We can let love guide our every thought and action, in all our relation-ships, in our communities, our work, our politics, and in all aspects of our being.

We all want a better life and a better world. It's love that makes life better. And it's love that can make our world better. *You* can make the world better. You can "Be the change that you want to see in the world".

Make love the meaning and purpose of your life. That's the answer to the problem of the human condition.

Love is the answer.

The answer to life is love.

The answer to life is love

You can change your life

We are all a product of our experience

If you treat people like good people, they will *be* good people

We are all on a journey

Changing the way we behave, changes us

The relationship is the therapy

We are meant to be connected

You can make a difference to every person you meet

We all need one another

A better world is possible

The answer to life is love

Exercise:

Learn the messages in this book. When you feel stuck, or frustrated, return to them.

References

1. **Harris, Nadine Burke.** How Childhood Trauma Affects Health across a Lifetime. *TED.* [Online] 2014. [Cited: 05 August 2020.] https://www.ted.com/talks/nadine_burke_harris_how_childhood_trauma_affects_health_across_a_lifetime/transcript?utm_source=tedcomshare&utm_medium=email&utm_campaign=tedspread#t-262256.

2. **Peterson, Jordan B.** *12 Rules For Life.* s.l. : Penguin Books, 2018.

3. **Van Der Kolk, Bessel.** *The Body Keeps the Score.* s.l. : Penguin Books, 2014.

4. **Walker, Pete.** *COMPLEX PTSD:From Surviving to Thriving.* s.l. : AZURE COYOTE, 2013.

5. **Frankl, Victor.** *Man's Search for Meaning.* Boston : Beacon Press, 1992.

6. **Southwick, Steven and Charney, Dennis**. *RESILIENCE: The Science of Mastering Life's Greatest Challenges.* Cambridge: Cambridge University Press, 2018.

7. **Samadder, Rhik.** *I Never Said I Loved You.* London : Headline Publishing Group, 2019.

8. **Carnegie, Dale.** *How to Win Friends and Influence People.* s.l. : Prabhat Books, 2008.

9. —. Maslow's Hierarchy of Needs. *Simply Psychology.* [Online] March 2020. [Cited: 05 August 2020.] https://www.simplypsychology.org/maslow.html#:~:text=Maslow's%20hierarchy%20of%20needs%20is,attend%20to%20needs%20higher%20up..

10. **Rogers, Carl R.** *On Becoming a Person.* London : Constable and Company, 1967.

11. **Santana, Rosa.** 5 Rhythms. *5 Rhythms.* [Online] 7 June 2019. [Cited: 7 June 2019.] 5 Rhythms.

12. **Cook, S.Ledger, K. Scott, N.** Dancing for Living. *Mental Health Foundation.* [Online] 2 January 2003. [Cited: 10 June 2019.] https://www.mentalhealth.org.uk/publications/dancing-living.

13. **McLeod, Saul.** Maslow's Hierarchy of Needs. *Simply Psychology.* [Online] 29 December 2020. [Cited: 22 04 2021.] https://www.simply-psychology.org/maslow.html#gsc.tab=0.

14. **Westacott, Emrys.** Nietzsche's Concept of the Will to Power. *ThoughtCo.* [Online] 25 05 2019. [Cited: 09 07 2019.] https://www.thoughtco.com/nietzsches-concept-of-the-will-to-power-2670658#the-will-to-power-as-a-psychological-principle.

15. **Cambell, Joseph.** *The Hero with a Thousand Faces.* New York : MJF Books, 1949.

16. **Aronson, Elliot.** *The Social Animal. Fifth Edition.* New York : W.H. Freeman and Company, 1988.

17. **Austin, Michael W.** The Habit Model of Moral Development. *Psychology Today.* [Online] 14 11 2014. [Cited: 09 07 2019.] https://www.psychologytoday.com/intl/blog/ethics-everyone/201411/the-habit-model-moral-development.

18. **Brooks, David.** *The Social Animal.* New York : Random House, 2011.

19. **Wilson, Timothy.** We Are What We Do. [book auth.] John Brockman (Ed). *This Explains Everything.* New York : Harper Collins, 2013, pp. 354-355.

20. **Cutler, C and HH Dalai Lama.** *The Art of Happiness.* s.l. : Hodder and Stoughton, 1998.

21. **Clarkson, Petruska.** *The Therapeutic Relationship. Second Edition.* London and Philadelphia : Whurr Publishers, 2003.

22. **Thomas Lewis, M.D., Fari Amini, M.D., Richard Lannon, M.D.** *A General Theory of Love.* New York : Vintage Books, 2001.

23. **Hari, Johann.** *Lost Connections.* London : Bloomsbury Publishing Plc, 2018.

24. **HH the Dalai Lama, Archbishop Desmond Tutu, and Douglas Abrams.** *The Book of Joy.* London : Hutchinson, 2016.

25. **Mineo, Liz.** Good Genes are nice, but Joy is Better. *The Harvard Gazette.* [Online] 11 April 2017. [Cited: 05 August 2020.] https://news.harvard.edu/gazette/story/2017/04/over-nearly-80-years-harvard-study-has-been-showing-how-to-live-a-healthy-and-happy-life/.

26. **The Human Connection Movement.** The Human Connection Movement. *The Human Connection Movement.* [Online] 05 August 2020. [Cited: 05 August 2020.] https://www.thehumanconnectionmovement.org.au/.

27. *Looking and loving: The effects of mutual gaze on feelings of romantic love.* **Kellerman, J. Lewis, L. and Laird, J.D.** 1989, Journal of Research in Personality, pp. 145-161.

28. Look Refugees in the Eye. *Amnesty International.* [Online] 24 05 2016. [Cited: 05 08 2020.] https://www.amnesty.org/en/latest/news/2016/05/look-refugees-in-the-eye/.

29. **Joines, Vann and Stewart, Ian.** *TA Today.* Kegworth, and North Carolina : Lifespace Publishing, 1987.

30. Sawubona: An African Tribe's Beautiful Greeting. *Exploring your mind.* [Online] 18 October 2018. [Cited: 10 May 2020.] https://exploringyourmind.com/sawubona-african-tribe-greeting/.

31. **Harari, Yuval Noah.** *Sapiens: A brief History of Humankind.* London : Vintage Books, 2014.

32. **Durkheim, Emile.** *The Division of Labour in Society.* Basingstoke : Palgrve Macmillan, 1984.

33. Fight Inequality Beat Poverty. *Oxfam.* [Online] 05 08 2020. [Cited: 05 08 2020.] https://www.oxfam.org.uk/get-involved/campaign-with-us/inequality-and-poverty.

34. **Ponciano, John.** The Changing Fortunes of the World's Richest. *Forbes magazine.* [Online] 23 May 2020. [Cited: 05 08 2020.] https://www.forbes.com/sites/jonathanponciano/2020/05/22/billion-aires-zuckerberg-bezos/#67277a6f7ed6.

35. **Wilkinson, Richard G.** *The Impact of Inequality.* London and New York : Routledge, 2005.

36. **Robinson, Sir Ken.** Do Schools Kill Creativity? *TED.* [Online] 2006. [Cited: 05 08 2020.] https://www.ted.com/talks/sir_ken_robinson_do_schools_kill_creativity/transcript?language=en.

37. **Zimbardo, Phillip.** *The Lucifer Effect.* London : Rider Books, 2012.

38. **Mitchell, David.** *Cloud Atlas.* London : Hodder and Stoughton, 2004.

39. **Pirsig, Robert M.** *Zen and the Art of Motorcyle Maintenance.* London : Vintage Books, 1974.

40. **Rogers, Carl R.** *A Way of Being.* New York : Houghton Mifflin Harcourt Publishing Company, 1980.

41. **Prabu, Dr. Joseph.** The Power and Urgency of the Golden Rule. *Parliament of the World's Religions.* [Online] 04 10 2019. [Cited: 06 08 2020.] https://parliamentofreligions.org/blog/2019-09-13-1201/power-and-urgency-golden-rule.

42. **Gandhi, Mahatma.** *An Autobiography: The Story of My Experiments With Truth.* s.l. : Courier Corporation, 1927.

43. **Mandela, Nelson.** *Long Walk to Freedom.* London : Abacus, 1995.

44. **King, Martin Luther.** *Strength to Love.* Boston : Beacon Press, 1963.

Printed in Great Britain
by Amazon